Fun-to-Learn
Bible Lessons:
Preschool, Volume 2

by Nancy Paulson

Loveland, Colorado

Fun-to-Learn Bible Lessons: Preschool, Volume 2
Copyright © 1995 Nancy Paulson

Credits
Book Acquisitions Editor: Mike Nappa
Editor: Paul Woods
Senior Editor/Creative Products Director: Joani Schultz
Copy Editor: Janis Sampson
Art Director: Kari Monson
Cover Art Director: Liz Howe
Cover Photographer: © 1989 Arthur Tilley, FPG International
Designer: Jill Christopher
Computer Graphic Artist: Bill Fisher
Illustrator: Jan Knudson
Production Manager: Gingar Kunkel

Unless otherwise noted, Scriptures quoted from The Youth Bible, New Century
Version, copyright © 1991 by Word Publishing, Dallas, Texas 75039. Used by permission.

Library of Congress Cataloging-in-Publication Data
    (Revised for volume 2)
Paulson, Nancy, 1947–
    Fun-to-learn Bible lessons.
    1. Bible—Study and teaching.   2. Preschool children—Conduct of life.
    3. Christian education of preschool children.   I. Title.
BS600.2.P385   1993   268'.432   93–35769
ISBN 1-55945-263-3 (v. 1)
ISBN 1-55945-602-7 (v. 2)

10 9 8 7 6 5 4   04 03 02 01 00 99 98
Printed in the United States of America.

Contents

Part 4: Look What Happens When People Pray!

Introduction

Welcome to a resource filled with lively, active Bible lessons for preschoolers. These are fun meetings that will hold your kids' attention and lay important foundations of faith.

In *Fun-to-Learn Bible Lessons: Preschool, Volume 2*, Sunday school teachers, vacation Bible school teachers, after-school program directors, and any leader of preschoolers will find 20 simple-to-follow lessons that teach children about prayer and worship. The lessons combine lively learning, colorful art projects, and scrumptious snacks to help kids learn a powerful point about prayer or worship each time.

The book is divided into these parts:

● **Part 1: Meeting God, Greeting God**—Preschoolers need to know God is approachable. We can pray anytime, about anything, and God will hear us.

● **Part 2: Getting to Know God**—Security in a relationship with God can be comforting to preschoolers. God knows what we need and will answer our prayers.

● **Part 3: Being Grateful**—Saying thank you is something most preschoolers learn early. They can also learn to be thankful to God.

● **Part 4: Look What Happens When People Pray!**—Preschoolers are strongly influenced by role models. These biblical examples demonstrate the power of prayer.

● **Fun-to-Learn Songs**—Give the song sheets on pages 94 and 95 to parents so children can sing their favorite songs at home. You can use the song sheets as a ready reference for class, too.

THE FUN-TO-LEARN BIBLE LESSONS

The lessons in *Fun-to-Learn Bible Lessons* each contain six to eight activities. Each activity lasts between three to 12 minutes. The activities are fast-paced and fun for children with short attention spans. Each lesson is divided into the following elements:

● **Introduction**—One or two paragraphs that give an overview of the lesson's topic.

● **A Powerful Point**—A short statement of the lesson's objective, telling you what children will learn.

● **A Look at the Lesson**—An outline including activity titles and estimated completion times. These times may vary depending on your class size.

● **The Fun-to-Learn Lesson**—Quick, active, reflective, Scripture-based activities. Lessons start with an opening experience to set the mood for the upcoming lesson. Kids experience the topics through active learning, using their senses of hearing, seeing, smelling, tasting, and feeling.

Lessons include interactive Bible stories, fun-filled rhymes and finger plays, songs to familiar tunes, art projects, and snacks.

● **Handouts**—All necessary handouts are included. They're easy to use, and you have permission to photocopy them for local church use.

Enjoy *Fun-to-Learn Bible Lessons: Preschool, Volume 2*. Use and adapt the Bible lessons for groups of any size. Watch kids develop self-esteem, meet new friends, and grow in their faith. And have fun teaching topics in an active, lively, and meaningful way!

Part 1: Meeting God, Greeting God

A God We Can Talk To

Who is God? What is prayer? How does God hear us? Children need to understand the answers to these basic questions before they can begin to develop a relationship with God. Preschoolers find it intimidating to speak to a God they can't see, and prayer is even more frightening in a group. Use this lesson to help children understand how we can pray and to help them feel comfortable talking to God.

A POWERFUL POINT

"Pray to me, and I will answer you. I will tell you important secrets you have never heard before" (Jeremiah 33:3).

Children will learn:

Prayer is talking to God, even though we can't see him.

A LOOK AT THE LESSON

1. Prayer Ball (5 to 10 minutes)
2. Prayer Train (3 to 5 minutes)
3. Where, When, What? (5 minutes)
4. Air and Prayer (5 to 10 minutes)
5. Learning to Pray (5 minutes)
6. What Does God Do? (10 minutes)
7. God Made Bananas (10 minutes)

THE FUN-TO-LEARN LESSON

1. Prayer Ball

(You'll need a small ball.)

When children have arrived, sit down on the floor with the children in a circle around you. Have the small ball ready in your hand. Ask:

- **Who is God?**
- **What is prayer?**
- Say: **God is here with us, even though we can't see him. Prayer is talking to God, even though we can't see him. I want to talk to God and thank him for each one of you.** Roll the ball to a child and say: **Thank you God for** (child's name)**. I am glad** (name) **could be here.** Then have that child roll the ball to the next child in the circle. Thank God for that child and continue until every child has had a turn.

Say: **God loves us and loves to have us talk to him.**

2. Prayer Train

Say: **Let's make a train and chug around the room. We're going to learn a rhyme that tells us Jesus loves you and me.**

Stand up and begin "chugging" around the room. Start saying the "Prayer-Train Rhyme" and invite the children to join you. Chug around the room several times, collecting the children into a line on your prayer train. When you get to the end of the rhyme, stop and have children turn around to the person behind them and say, "Thank you, God, for (child's name)."

Prayer-Train Rhyme

All aboard the prayer train!
(Start slowly.) **Chug-a-chug, chug-a-chug.**
(Faster) **Chug-a-chug, chug-a-chug.**
Chug-a-chug-a-choo-choo.
Jesus loves you!
Chug-a-chug-a-chee-chee.
Jesus loves me!
Up and down, up and down.
Jesus' love is all around!
(Repeat until all the children have joined the train.)
(Begin slowing down.) **Chug-a-chug, chug-a-chug.**
(Slower) **Chug-a-chug, chug-a-chug . . . Chooo.**

When children are sitting down, say: **Jesus is God. God loves us, and he loves to have us talk to him in prayer.**

3. Where, When, What?

Gather children together on the floor, and ask:
- **Can anyone tell me what prayer is?**
- **Where can we pray?**
- **When can we pray?**
- **What can we pray about?**

Say: **Now we're going to learn a new song that will help us know what prayer is. I will sing questions and answers first; then I will sing only the questions and you can sing the answers.**

This song is sung to the tune of "Three Blind Mice." Sing the song twice by yourself, then help kids begin singing the answers back to you. Sing through it until they begin to know the responses. Always sing the last line together.

Where, When, What? Song

Where do we pray?
Right here, anywhere!
When do we pray?
Right now, anytime!

What do we pray about?
All things without a doubt!
That's how we all can pray to God,
So let's pray now.

Say: **The last line of our song says, "So let's pray now." So let's pray now! Thank you, God, for our voices and for the fun we can have singing together. Amen!**
Say: **Even though we can't see him, God wants us to talk to him by praying. The Bible tells us a lot about prayer, and we're going to learn something about prayer from the Bible now.**

4. Air and Prayer

(You'll need a Bible.)
Present the Bible and say: **The Bible is a special book that teaches us how to pray. The Bible tells us that prayer is talking to God. God doesn't just live in heaven—he is here with us. God is everywhere. He hears everything we say. He loves to hear us talk to him. And we can talk to God, even though we can't see him.**

Prayer is as important to us as breathing. How long can you go without breathing?

Let children hold their breath until they have to let it out. Then say: **We need to pray just like we need to breathe. If we don't talk to God about things, we can feel bad—just like when we don't breathe. When we pray about things, it makes us feel better—kind of like taking a big, deep breath makes us feel better.**

God promises to hear and answer us when we pray.

Read aloud Jeremiah 33:3. Say: **God wants us to pray to him, even though we can't see him. We can pray to him anytime. He knows all about us and is just waiting for us to talk to him about our problems.**

5. Learning to Pray

Say: **Everyone stand up and stretch your hands toward heaven. Now pull the hair on your head. The Bible tells us God made every part of you, even every hair on your head! And he knows how many hairs each of us has.**

Hold up your hand if you have ever been to the beach and seen sand. Show me how you would fill a bucket with sand. Let children respond.

Then say: **The Bible tells us God even knows how many pieces of sand are on all the beaches in the world! If he knows all that, he must know a lot about us! He knows everything we do and everything we say. He hears us when we pray to him, even though we can't see him.**

When we pray, we think about God. Let's sit down and hear about a time Jesus taught people to pray.

Have children be seated on the floor as you open the Bible.

Say: **Clap your hands if you have ever heard about Jesus. He is the Son of God and when he talks to his Father in heaven he knows just what to say. Jesus' friends wanted to talk to God, too. They may have felt silly since they couldn't see God. Wiggle your feet if you feel silly sometimes.**

You can do what Jesus' friends did. They said, "Jesus, teach us to pray." Jesus was so happy to hear that. He wanted his friends to learn how to talk to God in heaven. Jesus is also our friend and wants us to talk to God anytime, anywhere, about anything. He taught his disciples to pray, and we can learn to pray, too. Prayer is talking to God, even though we can't see him.

Have children repeat the last sentence several times, then ask:
- **What is prayer?**
- **When can we talk to God?**
- **Where can we talk to God?**

Have children say, "Teach us to pray"—first loudly, then softly.

6. What Does God Do?

(Before class, make photocopies of the "What God Does" handout on page 12. Cut apart the sections on the page and place them in the paper bag. You'll also need construction paper and glue or tape.)

Say: **You can't see in this paper bag, but it's full of things God does. We can't see God, but we can see what he does.**

Let each child pick one section out of the bag then color and glue it onto the construction paper. Ask:
- **What do you see that God has done?**
- **What has God made in this picture?**

Say: **We can't see God, but we can see what he has made. Prayer is talking to him, even though we can't see him. We can tell God thank you for what he has made.**

7. God Made Bananas

(You'll need enough bananas to provide a 2-inch chunk for each child. Leave the peel on. Cut the bananas just before class or at the beginning of this activity.)

Show children a whole banana and say: **You can't see inside of this banana, but you know there is something good to eat inside. We can't see God, but we know he loves us and is good to us. We can't see God when we pray to him, but we know it is good to pray. Let's pray right now and thank God for making bananas for us.**

Help children pray a prayer of thanks. Then serve them 2-inch unpeeled sections of banana. Let the children peel and eat their bananas.

As children finish eating, say: **Prayer is talking to God, and he hears us even though we can't see him. I'm going to thank God right now for helping us learn about prayer today.**

Say a brief prayer of thanks to wrap up your class.

WHAT GOD DOES

God gives us flowers.

God makes animals.

God gives us families.

God makes mountains.

God makes lakes and oceans.

God gives us the sun.

The Best Book in the World

The foundation of our faith in God comes from the Bible. Most of what we know for sure about God we learned from studying the pages of Scripture. To be able to talk to God, we need to get to know him. And the way we get to know God is through the Bible. Young children can begin to learn about the Bible and how we can use it to learn more about God. Use this lesson to teach children the importance of the Bible.

A POWERFUL POINT

"All Scripture is given by God and is useful for teaching, for showing people what is wrong in their lives, for correcting faults, and for teaching how to live right" (2 Timothy 3:16).

Children will learn:

We can trust what the Bible tells us.

A LOOK AT THE LESSON

1. Jump In (5 to 10 minutes)
2. Prayer Train (6 to 8 minutes)
3. Where, When, What? (5 to 7 minutes)
4. Look at Jesus (8 to 10 minutes)
5. I Can't See It (10 minutes)
6. Sing a Prayer (3 to 5 minutes)
7. Cereal Surprise (10 to 12 minutes)

THE FUN-TO-LEARN LESSON

1. Jump In

(You'll need a small chair or box.)

Say: **We're going to be learning about faith today.**

Ask if there are any volunteers who have enough faith to stand on a chair or box and jump off into your arms.

Then say: **I promise I'll catch you. If you believe me and jump off, then you have faith in what I say.**

Give each child the opportunity to jump into your arms. As you catch each one, say: **Thanks for having faith in me.**

When all children have jumped, say: **You had faith in me when you did what I told you to. I didn't let you get hurt, did I? We can have faith in what the Bible tells us to do, too...**

(**Teacher Note:** If you're unsure of your ability to catch all of the children in your class, enlist another adult helper to assist you in catching the children.)

2. Prayer Train

Gather children together in a circle with this transition song and chug around the room a few times, having all the children join the line.

Prayer-Train Rhyme

All aboard the prayer train!
(*Start slowly.*) **Chug-a-chug, chug-a-chug.**
(*Faster*) **Chug-a-chug, chug-a-chug.**
Chug-a-chug-a-choo-choo.
Jesus loves you!
Chug-a-chug-a-chee-chee.
Jesus loves me!
Up and down, up and down.

Jesus' love is all around!
(Repeat until all the children have joined the train.)
(Begin slowing down.) **Chug-a-chug, chug-a-chug.**
(Slower) **Chug-a-chug, chug-a-chug . . . Chooo.**

3. Where, When, What?

Say: **We can pray to God and ask him to help us understand what we read in the Bible.** Ask:
● **Where can we pray?**
● **When can we pray?**
● **What can we pray about?**
Say: **Let's sing about it!** Lead the children in this song. You sing the questions and lead the children in singing the answers.

Where, When, What? Song

(Sing to the tune of "Three Blind Mice.")
Where do we pray?
Right here, anywhere!
When do we pray?
Right now, anytime!

What do we pray about?
All things without a doubt!
That's how we all can pray to God,
So let's pray now.

Say: **Now we're going to pray and thank God for giving us the Bible. The Bible tells us that "All Scripture is given by God and is useful."** One way the Bible is useful is that it teaches us how to pray. When we read the Bible, we are listening to God. When we pray we are talking to God. God is right here with us.
We can't see God, but he sees and hears us. God loves to hear us talk to him. And I'm going to talk to him right now to thank him for the Bible.
Dear God, thank you for your special book, the Bible. It teaches us all about you. Help us to have faith in what the Bible tells us.

4. Look at Jesus

(Before class, slip a picture of a boat in the Bible as a bookmark.)
Say: **Now we're going to listen to a story from the Bible about some people and a boat ride.**
Open the Bible, show children the picture of the boat, and ask:
● **Who likes to play in the water?**
● **Have you ever gone for a boat ride?**
Say: **Our story is about some friends of Jesus who were crossing a big lake when a big storm came up. The wind was blowing very hard. Show me how the wind would blow and tip the boat.**
Have children rock from side to side. **Jesus' friends were getting very scared that the boat would tip over! Then they saw Jesus walking on top of the water. One of the men in the boat named Peter wanted to walk to Jesus on the water. He asked Jesus if he could walk to him. Jesus said "yes." Peter believed what Jesus said. He stepped out of the boat. Let's pretend we're Peter and believe what Jesus tells us. Stand up and show me how you would step out of the boat.** Let children respond.
Peter started to walk toward Jesus. With Jesus' help, he made it out to Jesus, then back to the boat. Peter had faith when Jesus told him he could walk on the water. He had faith in Jesus' words. The Bible is where we read about Jesus and about other things from God. The Bible is God's Word. We can trust the Bible the way Peter trusted Jesus' words. Ask:

● **Who did Peter trust?**
● **How did Jesus help Peter?**
● **Why can we trust Jesus' words?**
Say: **We can trust what the Bible says because it gives us Jesus' words.**

When we pray, we can be sure God hears our prayers because the Bible tells us so.

5. I Can't See It

(Before class, draw crosses on sheets of white paper with a white crayon. Place them throughout the Bible so that children can pull them out during class. You'll also need poster paint, paintbrushes and paint shirts, and newspapers to cover the table.)

Have a child take one sheet of paper from the Bible. Say: **It doesn't look like there's anything on this piece of paper. But I have drawn something on it that's something from the Bible. I hope you believe I'm telling you the truth. Please have faith in me.**

Place poster paint in containers on a table covered with newspapers. Have each child take one sheet of paper from the Bible. Give each child a paintbrush and a paint shirt. Tell children to paint over the paper only once with the paint. Have them start on one side and go straight across to the other side of the paper. The picture will appear as they paint. Ask:

● **What do you see on your papers?**
● **What do crosses represent?**
Say: **The Bible tells us Jesus died on the cross. We couldn't see the crosses before we painted because they were drawn on white paper with a white crayon. But they were there all the time. You had faith in me and found these crosses from**
the Bible. Sometimes people say things that aren't true. But we can always have faith in what the Bible says.**

6. Sing a Prayer

Tell the children to tug on their own hair.
Ask:
● **When you get a haircut, do you believe your hair will grow back?**
Say: **The Bible tells us that God knows how many hairs we have on our heads. God knows everything.**

Have children form pairs and say to each other, "God loves you so much that he remembers everything about you." Then continue:

God tells us lots of things in the Bible. We can always have faith in the Bible, and we can pray to God anytime because he is always with us.

Lead children in the following song.

I Can Trust

(Sing to the tune of "Mary Had a Little Lamb.")
**I can trust the Bible,
The Bible, the Bible.
I can trust the Bible
Because it is God's Word.**

Say: **It's great that we can trust what the Bible tells us, and we can tell God we are glad about that.**

Lead your class in praying: **Thank you, God!**

7. Cereal Surprise

(You'll need crisp rice cereal tightly packed in a gift-wrapped box.)
Show children the gift-wrapped box of cereal. Let them shake and smell it, then ask:
● **Do you think I just wrapped up**

an empty box to fool you?

● **Will you trust me if I say there really is something inside the box?**

Slowly open it while you say: **You trusted me, and we are going to find a good snack when we open this box. We can always open the Bible and know that it has something good inside for us. We can trust what the Bible tells us.**

Give each child some of the cereal for a snack.

When We're Sorry

Preschoolers know what it means to feel guilty when they've done something wrong. It's a privilege to have God so near that we can tell him our failures and know that God understands us, forgives us, and will free us from guilt (Psalm 103:12-14). Use this lesson to teach the children that we can get rid of the bad feelings of guilt by telling God we're sorry for the wrong things we do.

A POWERFUL POINT

"If we confess our sins, he will forgive our sins, because we can trust God to do what is right. He will cleanse us from all the wrongs we have done" (1 John 1:9).

Children will learn:

We can tell God we are sorry for our sins, and he will forgive us.

A LOOK AT THE LESSON

1. Sunk by Sin (10 minutes)
2. Guilt Balloon (5 to 10 minutes)
3. Prayer Train (3 minutes)
4. Where, When, What? (5 to 10 minutes)
5. Boat Bodies (3 minutes)
6. I'm Sorry (5 minutes)
7. Smooth Sailing (10 minutes)
8. Boat Treats (5 to 10 minutes)

THE FUN-TO-LEARN LESSON

1. Sunk by Sin

(You'll need to set out a large tub of water with a boat floating in it. Put the rocks next to the tub.)

As children arrive, greet them and let them push the boat around on the water. When you're ready to begin, point out the boat and the rocks and say: **These rocks can teach us about sin and confession. Sins are the wrong things we do. Confession is when we tell God we're sorry about them. We're like this boat.**

Hold up a rock and say: **These rocks are like sin in our lives. Watch what happens if they get into my boat.**

Name some sins as you drop rocks into the boat, such as "I hit my brother," "I wouldn't clean my room," "I wouldn't share my toys," "I bit my friend," or "I got mad at my sister."

As the boat sinks, look distressed and say: **Oh, I'm sunk! I went to the bottom. But if I confess and tell God the wrong things I've done, watch what happens.**

Repeat the sins, beginning each one with "I'm sorry Lord for (name the sin)," as you lift the rocks from the boat. When the rocks are all out, float the boat again. Offer the rocks to the children and encourage them to tell about wrongs things that will sink the boat again. After you've sunk the boat again, have children say they're sorry for the sins they mentioned as you remove the rocks and refloat the boat. Then ask:

● **Do you get mad sometimes?**
● **Have you ever said bad things such as "I don't like you" or "Go away"?**

Say: **Maybe you've even said bad words sometimes. When that happens, we feel bad. We call those bad feelings guilt. We feel guilty when we've done something we know is wrong. But God loves us and doesn't want us to feel bad. If we tell him about it, he will take away the bad feelings. The Bible says "If we confess our sins, he will forgive our sins." Can you tell God about a time when you did something wrong and it made you feel bad?** Let children respond.

Say: **We can tell God we are sorry for our sins, and he will forgive us. When he forgives us, he also takes away those bad feelings of guilt.**

2. Guilt Balloon

(You'll need a balloon.)

Sit on the floor with the children in a circle around you. Encourage them to tell God they're sorry for the wrong things they've done. As each wrong thing is mentioned, blow a breath into the balloon and hold it. Say: **I'm holding all these bad things we've done in this balloon.**

When the balloon gets full, say: **Now we're going to tell God we're sorry for our sins and ask for his forgiveness.**

Lead the children in praying: **Dear God, I'm sorry for my sins,** **and I ask for your forgiveness.**

After children have prayed, say: **When God forgives us, he takes away all the guilt and bad feelings.** Let go of the balloon as you say: **And now we're going to let all those bad feelings disappear into the air.**

When we pray and tell God we're sorry for our sins, he forgives us and takes away all those bad feelings.

3. Prayer Train

Gather children into a line with this transition song and march around the room several times.

Prayer-Train Rhyme

All aboard the prayer train!
(Start slowly.) **Chug-a-chug, chug-a-chug.**
(Faster) **Chug-a-chug, chug-a-chug.**
Chug-a-chug-a-choo-choo.
Jesus loves you!
Chug-a-chug-a-chee-chee.
Jesus loves me!
Up and down, up and down.
Jesus' love is all around!
(Repeat until all the children have joined the train.)
(Begin slowing down.) **Chug-a-chug, chug-a-chug.**
(Slower) **Chug-a-chug, chug-a-chug . . . Chooo.**

Gather children in a group and say: **Stop the train! Remember we can pray anytime and anywhere about anything. We can even tell God about the wrong things we do. Let's sing about prayer right here.**

4. Where, When, What?

(You'll need a Bible.)

Sing this song about prayer. You sing the questions and lead the children in singing the answers.

Where, When, What? Song

(Sing to the tune of "Three Blind Mice.")

Where do we pray?
Right here, anywhere!
When do we pray?
Right now, anytime!

What do we pray about?
All things without a doubt!
That's how we all can pray to God,
So let's pray now.

Present the Bible and say: **The Bible is our special book that teaches us how to pray. When we read the Bible we are listening to God. When we pray, we are talking to God. God is here with us right now. He hears everything we say and wants us to tell him about everything.**

Sometimes it's hard to tell God we've done something wrong. But Jesus is God. He understands and will help us feel better when we tell him about it.

Lead children in praying: **Thank you, God, for forgiving us and helping us feel better when we tell you we're sorry for our sins.**

5. Boat Bodies

Ask:

● **What can you tell me about what we did with the boats earlier?**

● **Who can tell me what would happen to a real boat in the water if it got all full of rocks?**

Say: **Let's be boats and float in the water. Lay down on the floor on your tummy and raise up your hands, legs, and head. Rock back and forth and pretend you're a boat floating and rolling on the water.**

After kids have "rolled on the water" for 15 seconds or so, have them sit up on the floor. Say: **We had fun rolling on the water like boats. But if we sank into the water, we'd feel really bad. When we sin, we have bad feelings of guilt. But if we tell God we are sorry for our sins, he will always forgive us.**

6. I'm Sorry

(You'll need the boat, popcorn, rocks, and tub of water.)

Gather the children around in a circle and say: **The Bible tells us about King David. Most of the time King David was a very obedient man. He loved God. But one time he did some wrong things and disobeyed God. Let's pretend our boat is King David and these rocks will be the wrong things he did.**

Drop a rock into the boat for each sin: **He did not tell the truth. He hurt people. He took things that didn't belong to him. He tried to hide the bad things he'd done.** Keep dropping rocks until the boat sinks.

Say: **When King David realized what he'd done, he was very sorry and told God he was sorry. He asked God to forgive him for the wrong things he'd done.**

Empty the boat and float it again. Say: **When you tell God you're sorry about the wrong things you've done, God takes them away and forgets about them forever.** Ask:

● **If you tell God you're sorry, will he help you feel better?**

Look at our boat. It's empty. But God doesn't want us to float through life empty. He wants to fill us up with good gifts like love, joy, and peace.

Take out a bag of popcorn and say: **God loves to take away our sins and give us good gifts. Let's pretend these pieces of popcorn are the gifts God has to give us. Watch what happens.**

Fill the boat to overflowing with the popcorn while repeating: **Love, joy, peace, patience, kindness, goodness, gentleness...See, we can fill our boat to overflowing with God's goodness, and the boat will not sink. God not only takes away the bad feelings of guilt when we're sorry for our sins, but he helps fill our lives with good things, too.**

7. Smooth Sailing

(Before class, gather for each child a small clump of modeling clay and a plastic banana-split dish. Make a 6-inch square paper sail for each child and put each child's name on a sail. You'll also need straws, tape, and a tub of water.)

Give each child a dish, straw, and paper sail. Have children color their sails, then help attach each child's sail to a straw. Push the straw into the piece of modeling clay in each boat. While children float their boats in the tub of water, say: **We're like boats.**

God wants us to float through life on top of the water. He doesn't want us to sink because we're loaded down with sins. Ask:

● **How do you feel when you've done something wrong?**

Say: **Show me a sad face. God can help us feel better. He can take away that sinking feeling. We can tell God we're sorry for our sins, and he will forgive us. Then we don't have to feel bad anymore. And we can ask God to help us so we don't get mad or say bad things or lie to people.**

8. Boat Treats

(You'll need the boats, paper towels, and popcorn.)

Say: **We can always pray and ask God for forgiveness when we do wrong things. He's always there to listen to our prayers. Isn't that great? Now we're going to have a snack and celebrate how great it is that we can pray to God and that he will forgive us.**

Help the kids remove the sails and wipe out their boats with paper towels. As you fill each boat with popcorn, say to each child: **God loves you so much that he's waiting to make you feel better after you do something wrong.**

Celebrate God's forgiveness as you eat popcorn together.

God Forgives and Forgets

As small children explore this big world, they often go their own way. And before long they realize that not everyone thinks they're wonderful! Loneliness and timidity can result from hearing "You were naughty again." Preschoolers need to learn that God doesn't keep track of our wrongdoings after we ask him to forgive us for them. Use this lesson to encourage children to ask God for forgiveness when they do wrong things.

A POWERFUL POINT

"I am the One who forgives all your sins, for my sake; I will not remember your sins" (Isaiah 43:25).

Children will learn:

God forgives and forgets the wrong things we do.

A LOOK AT THE LESSON

1. I Can't Remember (5 to 10 minutes)
2. God Isn't Puzzled (5 minutes)
3. Prayer Train (3 to 5 minutes)
4. Prayer Ball (5 minutes)
5. Prayer Air! (5 to 10 minutes)
6. Peter Is Forgiven (5 minutes)
7. God Makes Things Right (10 minutes)
8. Happy Crackers (10 minutes)

THE FUN-TO-LEARN LESSON

1. I Can't Remember

(You'll need a baby doll, diapers, baby bottles, baby clothes, and a baby blanket set out on a table.)

Ask:

● **Can you remember when you drank from a bottle or wore diapers?**

● **Can you remember wearing clothes that were this small?**

● **Can you remember your mom carrying you around in a little blanket like this?**

You needed lots of help to grow up. Ask:

● **Who fed you, got you dressed, and changed your diapers?**

You can ask your parents how many times they did these things for you, but I'll bet they'll say, "I can't remember."

Let the children play with the baby items while you say: **The Bible teaches us that God knows everything but will not remember the wrong things we've done. God says, "I am the one who forgives all your sins . . . I will not remember your sins." God knows about the wrong things we do, but he forgives us and forgets about them when we tell him we're sorry and ask for forgiveness.**

2. God Isn't Puzzled

(You'll need a puzzle.)

Show children the puzzle. Take it apart and spread the pieces across a table. Then let the children put it back together again. Help them as needed. When the puzzle is back together, say:

We put this puzzle together even

though it was in lots of pieces. When we do wrong things, it's like our lives are in lots of pieces. But God can fix our lives and put them back together just like we put this puzzle back together. Ask:

● **Do you remember where every puzzle piece was before we started putting them together?**

Say: **I don't remember where all the puzzle pieces were. And God doesn't remember our sins after he forgives us. All we have to do is pray to him and tell him we're sorry for what we did wrong.**

3. Prayer Train

Say: **Let's say our "Prayer-Train Rhyme" and pretend our train has a crooked wheel. Can you wiggle and chug around the room at the same time?**

Prayer-Train Rhyme

All aboard the prayer train!
(Start slowly.) **Chug-a-chug, chug-a-chug.**
(Faster) **Chug-a-chug, chug-a-chug.**
Chug-a-chug-a-choo-choo.
Jesus loves you!
Chug-a-chug-a-chee-chee.
Jesus loves me!
Up and down, up and down.
Jesus' love is all around!
(Repeat until all the children have joined the train.)
(Begin slowing down.) **Chug-a-chug, chug-a-chug.**
(Slower) **Chug-a-chug, chug-a-chug...Chooo.**

Say the "Prayer-Train Rhyme," then stop and say: **Let's fix our crooked wheel and chug** around the room one more time. We can forget we ever had anything wrong with our train.

After going through the song again, gather the children in a group and say: **Stop the train! Our train went a lot smoother after we fixed the wheel, didn't it? When we ask for forgiveness for our sins, God makes everything right with us, like we made everything right with our wheel. Remember, we can pray anytime and anywhere about anything. We can tell God about the wrong things we do, and he'll forgive us and forget all about those sins.**

4. Prayer Ball

(You'll need a ball.)

Gather the children in a circle on the floor and pass a ball around the circle. Roll the ball to the fourth child from you and have that child hold the ball up in the air. Say: **This is our praise ball. Every time someone holds our praise ball in the air, let's all say, "God forgives and forgets!"**

Have children help you count to four as they pass the ball around the circle. Make sure each child has a turn.

5. Prayer Air!

(You'll need a Bible with a balloon in it.)

Sing the following song.

Where, When, What? Song

(Sing to the tune of "Three Blind Mice.")
Where do we pray?
Right here, anywhere!
When do we pray?
Right now, anytime!

What do we pray about?
All things without a doubt!
That's how we all can pray to God,
So let's pray now.

Present the Bible and take out the balloon. Say: **We can listen to God when we read the Bible. That's the way we learn what God is like. When we learn about Jesus, we're learning about God because Jesus is God. In our story, we'll learn that Jesus forgave Peter and forgot about his sins, just like he forgets about *our* sins. Let's thank God for forgiving us for the wrong things we do.**

Lead children in prayer: **Dear God, thank you that you know every-thing, but you choose to forget our sins after we ask for forgiveness.**

Blow air into the balloon and say: **Think about all the air in this bal-loon as all the wrong things we do. Watch what happens when I let go of the balloon.** Let go of the balloon and have kids watch it fly around the room. Ask:

● **What happened to the air in that balloon?**

Say: **Just like the air in our bal-loon disappeared, our sins disap-pear when God forgives us.**

Starting with the child next to you, go around the circle and tell children by name that God loves them so much that he will forgive them whenever they ask for forgiveness.

6. Peter Is Forgiven

(You'll need a Bible.)

Open the Bible and say: **Let's lis-ten to God carefully so that we can learn more about our good friend, Jesus.** Ask:

● **Have you ever done something wrong and heard your friends say they won't play with you anymore?**

Say: **Show me how you would feel. Make very sad faces. Do you think you might even cry?**

Our Bible story is about a man named Peter, who was a good friend of Jesus. When Jesus was going to die on the cross, Peter got scared and said he didn't know Jesus. When Peter thought about what he had done, Peter felt very bad because Jesus was his best friend. Show me how sad you think Peter was. Let children respond.

Say: **When Jesus came back to life, he told Peter not to feel bad anymore. Jesus understood how Peter felt and let him know that he had forgiven him. When we ask for forgiveness, God forgives us for the bad things we do and forgets all about them.**

7. God Makes Things Right

(Draw a large heart on a sheet of white paper for each child. You'll also need construction paper, crayons, and glue sticks.)

Give each child a paper heart and show children a sample of a repaired heart as described here. Let each child color the heart and then tear it into four or five pieces. Give children con-struction paper and tell them to glue their heart pictures back together.

Say: **Sometimes we do wrong things and wreck something or hurt people's feelings. When we ask God for forgiveness, he will help us put things back together and will forget all about our sin.**

8. Happy Crackers

(You'll need crackers, peanut butter, and mini chocolate chips.)

Give each child a few crackers. Let

children put peanut butter on the crackers and make happy faces on them with the chocolate chips. Have children say together: "Thanks, God, for forgetting the wrong things we do."

God Loves to Hear Us Sing

Worship is an expression of gratitude to God. It is action and obedience. It is the purpose of life (Psalm 119:175). Preschoolers can worship God. Focusing on God's greatness helps us depend on his power. Use this lesson to teach children that they can show God how glad they are to know him.

A POWERFUL POINT

"Come, let's sing for joy to the Lord. Let's shout praises to the Rock who saves us. Let's come to him with thanksgiving. Let's sing songs to him, because the Lord is the great God, the great King over all gods" (Psalm 95:1-3).

Children will learn:
We're glad to know God.

A LOOK AT THE LESSON

1. Praise Power (10 minutes)
2. March and Sing (5 minutes)
3. Praise Ball (5 to 10 minutes)
4. Trumpet Prayers (5 minutes)
5. Ways to Worship (5 to 10 minutes)
6. A Merry March (5 to 10 minutes)
7. Make a Joyful Noise (10 minutes)
8. Trumpet Treats (10 minutes)

THE FUN-TO-LEARN LESSON

1. Praise Power

(You'll need building blocks and cardboard tubes.)

After greeting the children, invite them to help you build a wall with the building blocks.

Say: **Our story today is about a group of people who obeyed God and marched around a city with a wall around it playing their horns for God. Because the people obeyed him, God made the city wall fall down so the people could get into the city. The leader's name was Joshua. God told Joshua to have the people march and sing and play their instruments. God did the rest.**

Give children cardboard tubes to use as horns. If you don't have cardboard tubes, you can make a horn by rolling up paper and taping the roll together. You could even flare one end to make it look more like a real horn.

Have children march around the wall of blocks singing this song to the tune of "Pop! Goes the Weasel."

Fall, Wall!

All around the wall they marched.
Yes, Joshua led the people.
They heard God's call to make it fall.
Crash! Went the wall.

When you get to the end of the song, have children toot their horns and then shout through the cardboard tubes, "We're glad to know God!"

Choose two children to knock down the wall, and then have two or three rebuild the wall. Have children repeat the activity, letting different ones knock down the wall. Compliment each child on his or her part in shouting, knocking down the wall, or rebuilding it.

2. March and Sing

(You'll need rhythm instruments.)
Gather the children and say: **Let's be a parade! We can march and sing and play instruments. God loves to hear us sing that we're glad to know him.**

Pass out the rhythm instruments and march around the room singing "Jesus Loves Me." Have children switch instruments and repeat the song.

3. Praise Ball

(You'll need a ball.)
Sit down with the children in a circle and say: **Singing is a wonderful way to show God we love him. He loves to hear you sing. When the ball is rolled to you say, "Thank you, God, for my voice to sing with."**

Make sure every child gets the ball before you finish.

4. Trumpet Prayers

(You'll need a Bible and a horn.)
Present the Bible. Place a horn on top of it and say: **Today our Bible story tells us how God used horns instead of guns or swords to help Joshua win a battle. Joshua asked God for help by praying. We're glad to know about God because he helps us when we pray. I am going to blow this horn every time a prayer goes up to God. Let's thank God for helping us with the hard things we have to do.**

Dear Lord, thank you for helping us to learn how to tie our shoes and go to school and get our clothes on ourselves. Sometimes those are hard things to do.

Help each child thank God for one thing. After each one prays, blow the horn.

5. Ways to Worship

Say: **There are a lot of ways to pray and thank God. Singing and playing instruments are two of those ways.** Ask:
● **Where can we worship God?**
● **When can we worship God?**
We can worship God at any time and in any place. Stand up and do what I say. We can pray and worship when we are walking. Walk around the room. **We can pray and worship on our knees with our hands folded.** Kneel and fold hands. **We can pray and worship with our eyes closed and our heads bowed.** Fold hands, close eyes, and bow head. **We can pray and worship looking up to heaven with our arms raised.** Lift hands and look up. **We can pray and worship while we're resting on our beds.** Lay down on the floor. **We can also pray and worship when we sit quietly. Everyone come sit quietly for the story in our group area.**

6. A Merry March

(You'll need a Bible and horn.)
Open the Bible to Joshua 6. Say: **Our Bible story is about a man named Joshua. God told Joshua to lead his people around the city of Jericho. God was going to**

give Jericho to Joshua and his people. The city had walls around it so
people couldn't get in. God told
Joshua not to fight. He told the people to march around the city and
play their instruments. So they did.

I want you to help me finish this
story. We'll make a story song. When
I blow this horn, I want you to sing,
"Praise him, praise him!" Then I'll
tell you what happens next.

Practice with the children by blowing the horn once or twice and helping them sing. Then continue with the
story.

**Joshua and his people got up
early in the morning and marched
around the city.** Blow the horn and
have the children sing, "Praise him,
praise him!"

**The people did this for six days.
On the seventh day, they marched
around the city seven times.** Blow
the horn and have the children sing,
"Praise him, praise him!"

**When they blew their horns and
shouted thank you to God, all the
walls came down and the people
could get into the city.** Blow your
horn and have children sing, "Praise
him, praise him!" one more time.

7. Make a Joyful Noise

(Before class, cut curling ribbon into
pieces about 3 feet long, making one
piece for each child. Place two paper
plates together with the bottoms facing
out, and staple them together three-
fourths of the way around. Punch eight
holes at equal distances around the edge
of each pair of plates. Make one of these
for each child in your class. Photocopy
the "Plate Centers" handout on page 28
and cut out one plate center for each

child. You'll also need crayons, glue
sticks, beans, a funnel, and scissors.)

Give each child one of the plates
you've prepared. Have each child glue
a plate-center picture to one side. Have
children color their plates. Place a funnel into the narrow opening between
the two plates and let each child pour a
handful of beans into the funnel. Staple
the opening closed.

Help each child weave the piece of
ribbon through the holes of the plate,
starting at the top. Then tie a small
bell on the ribbon and curl the ribbon.
Have children make a joyful noise
unto the Lord!

Say: **We're glad to know about
God. We can worship him with our
music.**

8. Trumpet Treats

(You'll need Bugles brand snacks.)

Give each child seven Bugles
snacks and tell the children again
about Joshua and the people walking
around the city for seven days. Have
children pretend to blow their Bugles
in praise to God before they eat them.

PLATE CENTERS

LET'S SING FOR JOY
TO THE LORD!

LET'S SING FOR JOY
TO THE LORD!

Part 2: Getting to Know God

God Knows Best

We often tell children it's not polite to ask for things. But when it comes to prayer, there should be no limitations. Use this lesson to encourage the children to ask God for anything they need. God promises to give us everything we *need*, and he will hear your children's prayers.

A POWERFUL POINT

"Do not worry about anything, but pray and ask God for everything you need, always giving thanks" (Philippians 4:6).

Children will learn:

When we ask God, he gives us what we need.

A LOOK AT THE LESSON

1. It's God Calling (5 to 10 minutes)
2. Prayer Train (3 to 5 minutes)
3. Prayer in the Air! (5 to 10 minutes)
4. Needs or Wants (5 minutes)
5. I'm Thirsty (5 minutes)
6. Right Choices (5 to 10 minutes)
7. Love Is Just a Call Away (10 minutes)
8. Drink Up (10 minutes)

THE FUN-TO-LEARN LESSON

1. It's God Calling

(You'll need to have two telephones set out on a table.)

After the children arrive, let them pretend to make phone calls. Tell them what a good job they're doing with the telephones.

Then say: **God wants us to call him anytime and ask him about anything. We can't see people we talk to on the phone, but we call anyway. We can't see God, but we can call him anytime by praying. God is always there to answer.**

2. Prayer Train

Say: **All aboard the prayer train!** Begin collecting the children from around the room as you say the "Prayer-Train Rhyme."

Prayer-Train Rhyme

All aboard the prayer train!
(Start slowly.) **Chug-a-chug, chug-a-chug.**
(Faster) **Chug-a-chug, chug-a-chug.**
Chug-a-chug-a-choo-choo.
Jesus loves you!
Chug-a-chug-a-chee-chee.
Jesus loves me!
Up and down, up and down.
Jesus' love is all around!
(Repeat until all the children have joined the train.)
(Begin slowing down.) **Chug-a-chug, chug-a-chug.**
(Slower) **Chug-a-chug, chug-a-chug . . . Chooo.**

When the train stops, have children sit in a circle on the floor and say:

Today we can ask God for something we really want. I really want to ask God that you have a good time in our class today and learn that God will give us what we need.

Lead children in a brief prayer.

3. Prayer in the Air!

Ask:

● **How many of you have ever been in an airplane?**

● **Would you want to take a ride like that?**

● **Is God clear up in the sky with the planes?**

Let's sing about all the places we can pray because God is everywhere.

Where, When, What? Song

(Sing to the tune of "Three Blind Mice.")

Where do we pray?
Right here, anywhere!
When do we pray?
Right now, anytime!

What do we pray about?
All things without a doubt!
That's how we all can pray to God,
So let's pray now.

Say: **Today we can ask God for things. When we ask him, he will give us what we need.** Pray: **Thank you, God, for giving us what we need when we ask you for it.**

4. Needs or Wants

(You'll need a large paper bag filled with a variety of items such as toys; candy; apple; soap; a bottle of water; gum; and pictures to represent houses, people, health, work, TV, video games, cars, animals, love (heart), air to breathe, and sunshine.)

Show children your bag of items. Give them each a chance to choose something out of the bag. Discuss whether each item is something we really need or just want.

Say: **God has made this world for us and promises to give us everything we need. He loves us to ask him for things, but does that mean we get everything we want? God knows what is best for us even when we want things that wouldn't be good for us.**

Return all of the items to the bag.

5. I'm Thirsty

(You'll need a Bible.)

Open the Bible to John 4. **Our Bible story is about a woman who was getting a drink of water. Jesus was nearby, and he was thirsty. He didn't have anything to drink out of, so the woman shared her cup and water with Jesus.**

The lady was thirsty, but she also had a lot of problems. She needed Jesus' help. Jesus wanted to give her something better than water. He told her he was the Son of God, and he would like to help her with all of her problems. He wanted her to be able to go to heaven someday. She believed him and was so happy. Jesus gave the woman what she really needed.

Jesus wants to help us, too. We can ask him about anything, and he will be there to help. He will give us what we need when we ask him for it. When we believe Jesus is the Son of God, we will go to heaven and be with Jesus forever!

6. Right Choices

(You'll need the bag of items and two empty bags.)

Divide the children into two lines—a

"need" line and a "want" line. Place two empty paper bags across the room from them—a bag for "needs" and a bag for "wants." Stand in front of the two lines of children, holding the bag of items you used earlier. Pull out an apple or another food item and ask:

● **Is this something we really need or something we just want to have? If it is a need, shout, "I need it!"** Ask:

● **Do we need food to keep us strong and healthy?**

Have the child at the head of the "need" line take the apple, put it in the "need" bag and then return to the end of his or her line. Pull out a toy from the bag and ask:

● **Is this something we need or just want? If you just want it, yell, "I want it!"**

Have the person at the head of the "want" line put it in the "want" bag. Continue pulling out items and asking children if the item is a want or a need until each child has had a turn or until the bag is empty.

At the end of the game, have the two lines join together and march around the room saying, "God gives me what I need."

7. Love Is Just a Call Away

(Before class, run photocopies of the "It's God Calling" handout (p. 33) on heavy colored paper. Cut out each handout and make slits on the dotted lines of the phone body. Cut a 12-inch piece of yarn and tie a knot in each end.)

Give each child a phone body, receiver, and yarn to assemble the telephone. Help children staple yarn to the Xs on their telephones.

Say: **Have fun calling God about anything and everything!**

8. Drink Up

(You'll need chocolate milk, cups, and ice cream.)

Give each child a half cup of chocolate milk. Help children scoop softened ice cream into the milk. Talk about the lady who was thirsty and shared her water with Jesus. Remind children that Jesus gave her something better than water.

Say: **Jesus gave that lady the free gift of life forever in heaven. We can have that gift, too. She believed that Jesus was God's Son, and so do we!**

IT'S GOD CALLING

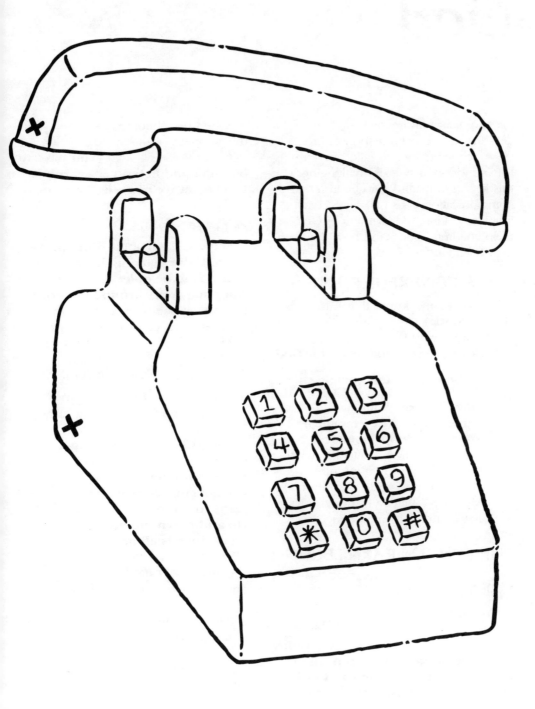

We Can Hear God

Conversation becomes meaningful when we get a response. Pre-schoolers love to talk, but learning to wait for an answer is challenging. Use this lesson to teach your children that communication goes two ways. Prayer involves talking and listening to God. Help children understand how they can hear from God.

A POWERFUL POINT

"Be quiet and know that I am God" (Psalm 46:10a).

Children will learn:
We can be quiet and listen for God.

A LOOK AT THE LESSON

1. Quiet Friends (5 minutes)
2. Prayer Train (3 to 5 minutes)
3. Time Out (5 to 10 minutes)
4. Listen to the Lyrics (5 to 10 minutes)
5. Prayer Air! (5 to 10 minutes)
6. God Whispers (5 to 10 minutes)
7. My Prayer Place (10 minutes)
8. Eat Quietly (10 minutes)

THE FUN-TO-LEARN LESSON

1. Quiet Friends

(You'll need a puppet.)

As the children arrive, greet them with the puppet. Then whisper: **Today we're learning about listening to God. My puppet friend can't talk. He can only listen. Tell him "hello" and see what he does.**

When the children say "hello," have the puppet nod his head.

Continue to whisper: **You have to be quiet and listen very carefully to hear what we're going to do next.**

2. Prayer Train

Softly say: **All aboard the prayer train. We're learning how important it is to be quiet. Let's see if we can chug softly around our room.** Have everyone whisper the rhyme and chug on their tiptoes until they're gathered in a circle on the floor.

Prayer-Train Rhyme

All aboard the prayer train!
(Start slowly.) **Chug-a-chug, chug-a-chug.**
(Faster) **Chug-a-chug, chug-a-chug.**
Chug-a-chug-a-choo-choo.
Jesus loves you!
Chug-a-chug-a-chee-chee.
Jesus loves me!
Up and down, up and down.
Jesus' love is all around!
(Repeat until all the children have joined the train.)
(Begin slowing down.) **Chug-a-chug, chug-a-chug.**
(Slower) **Chug-a-chug, chug-a-chug...Chooo.**

Stop the train with the children in a circle. Have them sit down right where they are.

Say: **Remember, we can pray anytime and anywhere about anything. When we pray we can listen for what God wants us to know, too.**

3. Time Out

(You'll need a kitchen timer and a ball.)

Show children the kitchen timer and ball. Say: **Today we're learning about listening. To listen, we must be very quiet and not talk. Sometimes it's very hard to be quiet. Let's see if we can be perfectly quiet for 30 seconds.**

Set the timer for 30 seconds and remain quiet. If kids have trouble being quiet, reset the timer and try again.

When they've been quiet until the timer goes off, say: **Thirty seconds can seem like a long time. But we can stay quiet and think about what God might want us to know.**

I'm going to tell (child's name to your right) **a secret.** (Child's name) **will whisper it to the next person, and we'll all tell it to the person next to us until it goes all the way around the circle and back to me. I will tell you if what I heard is what I said. Sit still and listen carefully to try and get it right.**

Whisper a simple sentence such as "I like to have ice cream with my apple pie" to the first child and let the message go around the circle. Have the last child say aloud what he or she heard. Then tell children what you said to the first child. Ask:

● **Why was the message different at the end?**

Say: **Sometimes it's hard to hear each other even when we're really trying to listen. Sometimes it's hard to know what God wants to say to us, too. But we can be quiet and listen for him.**

Roll the ball to one student. Whisper: **Here's a quiet message from me: God loves you and I do, too.** Have that student roll the ball to the next person in the circle and repeat your message to that child. Let the message go all the way around the circle.

4. Listen to the Lyrics

Go through this activity several times, saying the silly rhyme loudly and then softly. Form two groups. Have one group listen while the other group says it with you. Or have groups run with you from one side of the room to say the rhyme and then run to the other side and say it.

Hi Daddle Doodle

Hi daddle doodle (wave both arms)
With a flip, flap, floodle (clap hands)
And a snip, snap, snoodle (snap fingers)
And a du-datchi, du-datchi (slap knees)
Du, du, du! (Stomp feet.)

After you have tried doing the rhyme several ways, ask:

● **Words can be funny, can't they? What do we call words when we talk to God?** Let children respond.

Say: **Let's sit down and sing about talking to God.**

5. Prayer Air!

(You'll need a Bible with a balloon in it.)

Have children sit down, then say: **Sing very softly so that we can listen to God, too.**

Where, When, What? Song

(Sing to the tune of "Three Blind Mice.")

Where do we pray?
Right here, anywhere!
When do we pray?
Right now, anytime!

What do we pray about?
All things without a doubt!
That's how we all can pray to God,
So let's pray now.

Open the Bible and take out the balloon. Say: **Let's pretend that the air I blow into this balloon is all the things we want to say to God.**

Inflate the balloon. Ask:

● **What will happen when I let go of the balloon?**

Say: **When I let go of this balloon all the air will come out, just like when we pray to God and all our words come out.** Let go of the balloon. When it stops, point to it and ask:

● **What's the balloon doing now?**

Say: **After we pray, we can be quiet like the balloon is quiet, and we can listen to God. Sometimes he reminds us of things we have learned about from the Bible.**

6. God Whispers

(You'll need a Bible, candle, and matches.)

Dim the lights and light the candle. Open the Bible to 1 Kings 19. Tell the story quietly, emphasizing that we hear God when we read the Bible.

Say: **Our Bible story is about a man named Elijah. He worked very hard for God, prayed a lot, and tried to do what God wanted. But sometimes he had trouble knowing what God wanted him to do.**

Elijah left the noisy city and went to listen for God in a quiet place. He went up a mountain and into a cave, but it wasn't quiet there because a

great big storm came up. The wind blew, the rain fell, and the trees shook. Elijah was scared! Raise your hand if you would be scared. What do you think Elijah did?

He prayed to God. God answered Elijah's prayer and made the storm go away. A soft, quiet breeze went by and Elijah heard what God wanted him to know. We can remember to pray, too. Pretend you are like a soft, little breeze and blow out our candle.

Have children gently blow out the candle. Turn up the lights.

7. My Prayer Place

(You'll need the candle, matches, and kitchen timer.)

Say: **If we listen to God when we pray, he can help us think of things from the Bible that will help us. But we need to be quiet and listen. Let's sing a song about listening for God.**

I Will Listen

(Sing this song to the tune of "Frère Jacques.")

I will listen. I will listen.
God is near. God is near.
We can listen for him. We can
    listen for him.
We will hear. We will hear.

After singing, dim the lights and light the candle again. Set the timer for 30 seconds.

Say: **I'm going to pray. Let's be quiet and think about things we have learned from the Bible. God might have something he wants us to remember.** Pray: **Thank you, God, that we can pray and you listen to us. Help us to listen for what you might say to us.**

Have children sit quietly and listen to God. When the timer goes off, ask if anyone would like to share something about God that they have learned from the Bible. Turn up the lights and blow out the candle.

8. Eat Quietly

(You'll need cereal, bowls, and milk.)

Give each child a bowl of crisp rice cereal and say: **We have to be good listeners to hear God. He speaks quietly and won't ever yell at us. We can be quiet and listen for God. When I put the milk on your cereal, you have to be a real good listener to hear the little crackling sounds it will make. As I pour the milk, listen to the cereal snap and pop. If you can hear it, you're a good listener.**

Let children listen for the popping sounds, then have them eat their cereal.

At Your Service, God

Preschoolers want to please the people in their world. They gain confidence as they receive signs of approval. Learning to make right choices is a lifetime process, and the Bible can help us in making those choices. Use this lesson to help preschoolers learn that living the Christian life means doing the things God wants us to do.

A POWERFUL POINT

"My God, I want to do what you want. Your teachings are in my heart" (Psalm 40:8).

Children will learn:

We want to do what God wants us to do.

A LOOK AT THE LESSON

1. A Safe Place to Be (5 minutes)
2. Walking Right (5 minutes)
3. Prayer Train (3 to 5 minutes)
4. Our Guide Book (5 minutes)
5. Prayer Air! (5 to 10 minutes)
6. Jesus Obeyed (5 to 10 minutes)
7. Follow Directions (10 minutes)
8. Fruit Favorites (10 minutes)

THE FUN-TO-LEARN LESSON

1. A Safe Place to Be

(You'll need a fish in a fishbowl.)

Greet the children and say: **Today we're learning about doing what God wants us to do.**

Look at this fish in the water. What would happen to him if he jumped out of the water? Yes, it would die. God made a special plan for you and me just like he made fish to live in the water. To please God, we need to do what he wants us to just like this fish needs to stay in the water to live.

2. Walking Right

Say: **God planned for us to walk forward. We can walk backward, but it's hard to do. Try walking backward.** Pause for children to respond. **Now go forward.** Pause for children to respond once more. Then ask:

- **Which one do you like best?**
- **Can you run backward?**
- **Can you run forward?**

Let children run forward and backward for a few seconds. Be sure to have children spread out so they don't run into each other.

Say: **Wasn't that fun? God loves to see us have fun. Isn't it fun to do what God wants us to?**

3. Prayer Train

Let's walk around the room on our prayer train. A train needs to stay on the track to keep going. We need to stay on track with God's plan. We stay on track when we read the Bible and do what it tells us.

38

Prayer-Train Rhyme

All aboard the prayer train!
(Start slowly.) **Chug-a-chug, chug-a-chug.**
(Faster) **Chug-a-chug, chug-a-chug.**
Chug-a-chug-a-choo-choo.
Jesus loves you!
Chug-a-chug-a-chee-chee.
Jesus loves me!
Up and down, up and down.
Jesus' love is all around!
(Repeat until all the children have joined the train.)
(Begin slowing down.) **Chug-a-chug, chug-a-chug.**
(Slower) **Chug-a-chug, chug-a-chug . . . Chooo.**

Gather the children in a group and say: **Stop the train! We can learn from the Bible what God wants us to do. And we can stay on the right track when we do what the Bible tells us.**

4. Our Guide Book

(You'll need a Bible and a TV schedule guide.)

Gather the children into a circle on the floor. Show them the TV schedule guide and say: **This book helps us know what we can watch on TV each day.**

Now show them the Bible and say: **The Bible helps us know what is right and wrong for our lives. It's God's special book to help us know what he wants us to do. We had fun running forward because that's the way God wants us to run. We can have fun doing more things God's way as we learn more things God wants us to do.**

5. Prayer Air!

(You'll need a Bible with a balloon inside.)

Remove the balloon from the Bible and ask:

● **Can I blow up this balloon with my nose? Why not?**

Say: **Air comes out of my nose just like it comes out of my mouth, but I can't use my nose to blow up this balloon. The balloon was made to be blown up by someone's mouth.**

Sometimes we try to do things differently than God intended, and that causes us trouble.

Let's sing and then pray to ask God to let us know what he wants us to do.

Where, When, What? Song

(Sing to the tune of "Three Blind Mice.")
Where do we pray?
Right here, anywhere!
When do we pray?
Right now, anytime!

What do we pray about?
All things without a doubt!
That's how we all can pray to God,
So let's pray now.

Pray: **Dear God, we want to please you. Help us to always know what you want us to do.**

6. Jesus Obeyed

Say: **Sometimes it isn't easy to do what God wants us to. It was hard for Jesus to die on the cross. But he came back to life for us so we could go to heaven and live with him forever. We can go to heaven because Jesus did what God wanted him to do.**

When we do what God wants us to, it pleases God. Ask:

● **Have you ever been sick and had to take medicine to get better?**

Say: **Sometimes medicine doesn't taste very good, but it's important to obey your parents and take it. When you listen to your parents, you are doing what God wants. And that pleases him.**

7. Follow Directions

(Before class, put tape on the ends of 2-foot lengths of string for each child. Tie a cereal loop on one end of each length of string. Make a sample necklace with a simple pattern of three Froot Loops and one rigatoni noodle, then three more Froot Loops. You'll also need bowls of Froot Loops and rigatoni noodles.)

Show your sample necklace to the children and ask:

● **Do you like my necklace?**

● **Would you like to have one just like it?**

Say: **If you choose to, you can make one just like mine. If we choose to, we can do what God wants us to. We can choose to follow Jesus and obey God the way he did.**

Give a piece of string to each child and place bowls of mixed Froot Loops and rigatoni noodles on the tables.

Say: **The cereal is all mixed up with the noodles. You will have to look it over and choose one at a time. Sometimes we get mixed up and have a hard time knowing what God wants. We have to carefully choose what God wants us to do.**

If you would like me to help you with your necklaces, I will. God will always help us when we need it, too.

As you help children with their necklaces, affirm each child for his or her beautiful creation.

8. Fruit Favorites

(You'll need apple slices, orange sections, fresh Froot Loops cereal, and paper towels.)

Serve apple slices and orange sections with fresh cereal and ask:

● **Where does fruit grow?**

Say: **God's plan for fruit trees is to produce fruit. When fruit trees produce fruit, they are doing what God wants them to. God has different things that he wants us to do. We can learn from the Bible what God wants us to do, and we can do it. That pleases God and will make us happy, too.**

Partner Power

It's easy to end a prayer with "in Jesus' name" and not really think about what that means. But praying in Jesus' name is more than saying those words. It's focusing on what Jesus has done for us, and acknowledging that only through him can our prayers ever be heard and answered. Preschoolers can learn that Jesus is our partner in prayer.

A POWERFUL POINT

"And if you ask for anything in my name, I will do it for you so that the Father's glory will be shown through the Son" (John 14:13).

Children will learn:

Our prayers are answered by the power of Jesus.

A LOOK AT THE LESSON

1. What's Your Name? (5 to 10 minutes)
2. Prayer Train (3 to 5 minutes)
3. Prayer Air! (5 to 10 minutes)
4. Peter's Powerful Prayer (5 to 10 minutes)
5. Thankful Hands (10 minutes)
6. Helpful Hands (10 minutes)

THE FUN-TO-LEARN LESSON

1. What's Your Name?

(You'll need a book of name definitions.)
Look up the meaning of names in the name book. Be prepared to tell your students what their names mean.

Then say: **In Bible times, names were very important. They told a lot about a person.** Ask:
● **Have you ever heard people end a prayer by saying, "in Jesus' name, amen"?**
Say: **Praying in Jesus' name is saying that it is because of Jesus that we can pray to God. The "amen" means you are saying, "Yes, I believe in Jesus' power."**

2. Prayer Train

Gather children together with the "Prayer-Train Rhyme." Ask them to say "amen" with you when your train stops.

Prayer-Train Rhyme

All aboard the prayer train!
(*Start slowly.*) **Chug-a-chug, chug-a-chug.**
(*Faster*) **Chug-a-chug, chug-a-chug.**
Chug-a-chug-a-choo-choo.
Jesus loves you!
Chug-a-chug-a-chee-chee.
Jesus loves me!
Up and down, up and down.
Jesus' love is all around!
(*Repeat until all the children have joined the train.*)
(*Begin slowing down.*) **Chug-a-chug, chug-a-chug.**
(*Slower*) **Chug-a-chug, chug-a-chug . . . Chooo.**
Amen.

Gather the children in a group and say: **Remember, we can pray anytime**

and anywhere about anything.
And when we pray in Jesus'
name, we're saying that it's only
through Jesus' power that God
hears and answers our prayers.

3. Prayer Air!

(You'll need a Bible with a balloon in it.)

Sing the following song together.

Where, When, What? Song

(Sing to the tune of "Three
Blind Mice.")
Where do we pray?
Right here, anywhere!
When do we pray?
Right now, anytime!

What do we pray about?
All things without a doubt!
That's how we all can pray to God,
So let's pray now.

Present the Bible and remove
the balloon, then say: **Jesus is like**
our partner when we pray. And
he can help us understand what
the Bible says, too. It's good to
ask Jesus to help us do what the
Bible tells us to do. Jesus wants
to be our helper. Let's thank
him today for helping us with
our prayers. We can ask him to
help us do what the Bible says.

Pray: **Thank you, God, for giv-**
ing us Jesus so that we can pray
to you. In Jesus' name, amen.

Inflate the balloon and say: **We**
can't see the air that's in this bal-
loon, but we know it's there. We
also can't see Jesus, but he's al-
ways with us as our partner. Our
prayers are answered through
his power.

4. Peter's Powerful Prayer

(You'll need the Bible.)

Open the Bible to Acts 3:1. Say:
Our story is about a man named
Peter who was going to worship
one day when he saw a man sit-
ting on the steps. The man could-
n't walk. He had never been able
to walk. He was asking people for
money because he had no way to
earn it. When he saw Peter he
asked him for money, too. He
stuck out his hand hoping Peter
would give him money. But Peter
said to the man, "I don't have
money for you, but I have some-
thing much better."

Then Peter prayed, "By the
power of Jesus you can walk!"
Peter pulled the man up by his
hand, and the crippled man
began to walk and jump. He was
so excited and happy! He start-
ed praising God and showing
everyone what God had done
for him.

Everyone take the hand of the
person sitting next to you and
help pull that person up so we
can go to our tables and make a
thankful hand.

5. Thankful Hands

(Before class, make photocopies
of the "Heart for Prayer" handout on
page 44. Cut the hearts out. Prepare
a 1-foot piece of yarn for each child
by tying a knot in each end. You'll
also need plain paper, crayons, and
a stapler.)

Gather the children at tables.
Give each one a sheet of paper
and a heart. Help them trace
around their hands on their
papers. Then have children color
their hearts and their papers. Help
each child connect the two papers

by stapling one end of the yarn to the heart and the other end to the hand outline.

Say: **Jesus loves to give us a helping hand when we pray.**

6. Helpful Hands

(You'll need a jar of raisins.)

Make sure the lid is secure on your jar of raisins. Put the jar in the center of a circle on the floor. Gather the children around the jar and ask:

● **Would you like to eat these raisins for our snack today?**

Say: **You can have them if you can get the jar open with one hand. Hold one hand behind you and try to open this jar. It has to stay on the floor in the circle.**

Let a volunteer try. Say: **I guess you will need to ask me for help. I can use one hand to help you. Together I bet we can open the jar.**

Hold the jar securely while the child turns the lid. Say: **Jesus wants to help you pray just like I wanted to help you open this jar. Because of Jesus, God hears and answers our prayers.**

Tell each child: **Jesus will answer your prayers.**

Give children a handful of raisins. Together, pray: **Thank you, God, for this snack. In Jesus' name, amen.**

HEART FOR PRAYER

My Important Job

An ambulance went by. A small child's eyes grew large at the sound and the sight. Then he immediately began to pray for the sick person inside the ambulance.

Spontaneous "arrow" prayers to God can be a response preschoolers develop as they learn the freedom of talking to God anytime about anything. Use this lesson to encourage the children to pray for other people.

A POWERFUL POINT

"First, I tell you to pray for all people, asking God for what they need and being thankful to him. Pray for rulers and for all who have authority so that we can have quiet and peaceful lives full of worship and respect for God" (1 Timothy 2:1-2).

Children will learn:
Jesus wants us to pray for others.

A LOOK AT THE LESSON

1. Prayer Friends (5 to 10 minutes)
2. Prayer Air! (5 to 10 minutes)
3. Finger Prayers (5 to 10 minutes)
4. Power Prayers (5 minutes)
5. Prayer for Others (5 to 10 minutes)
6. Sharing Is Caring (5 to 10 minutes)

THE FUN-TO-LEARN LESSON

1. Prayer Friends

(You'll need a ball.)

Have children sit in a circle and let them roll the ball to one another. Each time a child receives the ball, say: **Being a friend can mean praying for each other.** Have the child receiving the ball say, "Thank you, God, for my friend (name)."

After a few minutes of play, say: **Jesus wants us to pray for others. He cares about our friends like we do. And he wants us to talk to him about people who need help.**

2. Prayer Air!

(You'll need a Bible with a balloon in it.)

Say: **Remember, we can pray anytime and anywhere about anything. We can pray for our friends and for people who need help.**

Sing the following song together.

Where, When, What? Song

(Sing to the tune of "Three Blind Mice.")
Where do we pray?
Right here, anywhere!
When do we pray?
Right now, anytime!

What do we pray about?
All things without a doubt!

45

That's how we all can pray to God, So let's pray now.

Present the Bible and open it to 1 Timothy 2:1-2.

Remove the balloon from the Bible and say: **Jesus wants us to pray for others. He wants us to pray for our friends and for our country's leaders.**

Hold up the balloon. Ask:

● **What can this balloon do by itself?**

Inflate the balloon. Ask:

● **Now what can this balloon do?**

Say: **Now that we've put air in this balloon, I can let it go, and it can fly around the room.**

Let go of the balloon. When it stops, say: **When we put air in the balloon, we made it able to fly around the room. When we pray for people, God can help them do good things.**

3. Finger Prayers

(Before class, make copies of the "Praying Hands" handout on page 48.)

Give each child a copy of the "Praying Hands" handout.

Say: **Our hands can help us pray. We can fold them when we pray. Show me how we fold them. Now hold up one hand and let's use it like this hand in our picture. Our hands can help us remember who to pray for.**

Continue by explaining how each finger can help us pray for certain people.

Say: **I want to teach you a rhyme to help us remember who to pray for.**

Go through the rhyme once by yourself. Then have children try to say it with you. Go over it with them at least two more times.

Helping-Hands Rhyme

See my hands. They help me so.
(Hold up both hands.)
Wiggly fingers—watch them go!
(Wiggle fingers.)

When I talk to God, I pray.
Each one tells me what to say.
(Fingers of one hand touch the other hand.)

Thumbs are, oh, so close to me.
(Touch thumbs to chest.)
I'll pray for my family.

Pointer tells me what to do.
(Shake index finger.)
I'll pray for my teacher, too.

Middle stands so tall, not bent.
(Hold one hand upright and hold the other hand flat over it.)
I'll pray for the president.

This one likes to wear a ring.
(Hold up fourth finger.)
For the sick and weak, I'll sing.

Little finger—small to see.
(Wiggle pinkie.)
Now, I think, I'll pray for me.

See, my hands—they help me so. *(Fold hands in prayer.)*
Fold together with heads bowed low.

Say: **Jesus wants us to pray for others. And this little rhyme will help us remember who to pray for.**

4. Power Prayers

(You'll need the Bible.)
Open the Bible to Acts 12.

Say: **Our Bible story is about a man named Peter. Peter loved God very much, and he loved to tell people about Jesus. But some men thought Peter was telling lies (things that aren't true), so they had Peter put in jail.**

They put chains on him so he couldn't get away. They had soldiers watching him all the time. But Peter had a lot of friends who were praying for him. God heard their prayers and sent an angel right into the jail. Let's pretend we're Peter. Show me what you would do when the angel appeared in the jail.

The angel tapped Peter on the shoulder and said, "Get up and come with me." When Peter stood up, all the heavy chains fell off, and he headed toward the door with the angel.

Peter was afraid of the guards. If they saw him, they would grab him. But Peter's friends were praying for him. Peter and the angel walked right by the guards, and no one saw them. They went out the door perfectly safe.

Jesus wants us to pray for others, like Peter's friends prayed for him. God answers prayers and takes care of us, just like he answered Peter's friends' prayers.

5. Prayer for Others

(Before class, make copies of the "I Can Pray for Others" handout on page 49. Cut open the door. You'll also need crayons, scissors, and paper fasteners.)

During class give each child a copy of the "I Can Pray for Others" handout to color. Assist each child in cutting out the circle and attaching it with a paper fastener to the X on the page. Encourage each one to spin the circle and choose a person to pray for. Help them pray for the people they've chosen.

6. Sharing Is Caring

(You'll need the raisins, nuts, dried fruit, cereal, and napkins.)

Give each child a large napkin. Provide raisins, nuts, dried fruit, and cereal. Let children put a variety of finger food on their napkins. Have children each fold the napkin up and give it to the person next to them.

Say: **Praying for someone is like giving that person a special treat. When we care about people, we like to pray for them. Jesus wants us to pray for others. He cares about people even more than we do.**

PRAYING HANDS

I CAN PRAY FOR OTHERS

I can pray for others.

Part 3: Being Grateful

Thank You Notes to God

"Thank you" is one of the first phrases most parents teach a child. Preschoolers learn very early that they are praised for saying "thank you." They also enjoy hearing "thank you" when they have been helpers.

Use this lesson to show children how pleased God is to hear them tell him "thank you."

A POWERFUL POINT

"I will praise you, Lord, with all my heart. I will tell all the miracles you have done. I will be happy because of you; God Most High, I will sing praises to your name" (Psalm 9:1-2).

Children will learn:

Saying "thank you" to God shows God we love him.

A LOOK AT THE LESSON

1. Thanks to God (5 to 10 minutes)
2. Prayer Train (5 minutes)
3. Prayer Air! (5 to 10 minutes)
4. Color Prayers (5 minutes)
5. Hannah Was Happy (5 minutes)
6. Thank You Balloons (5 to 10 minutes)
7. Flowers of Thanks (5 to 10 minutes)

THE FUN-TO-LEARN LESSON

1. Thanks to God

(Before class, tape a large sheet of butcher paper on the wall with the caption "Thank you, Jesus!" across the top. Have chalk, colored markers, crayons, and stickers available.)

As children arrive say: **Today we're going to make a thank you note to God for all the wonderful things he does for us. You can draw something you are thankful for on this paper. It will be our giant thank you to God.**

Let children work together to decorate the paper. Ask them to tell you about their drawings.

When everyone has had a chance to contribute to the thank you poster, remove it from the wall, roll it up, and tie a ribbon around it.

Say: **Wouldn't it be great if we could send this up to heaven? But we don't have to do that because God is here with us. God has already seen every picture you drew for him! And each one of you drew such a wonderful picture! I'm sure our note pleased him very much.**

2. Prayer Train

Collect the children together by using the prayer-train activity.

Prayer-Train Rhyme

All aboard the prayer train!
(*Start slowly.*) **Chug-a-chug, chug-a-chug.**
(*Faster*) **Chug-a-chug, chug-a-chug.**
Chug-a-chug-a-choo-choo.
Jesus loves you!
Chug-a-chug-a-chee-chee.

51

Jesus loves me!
Up and down, up and down.
Jesus' love is all around!
*(Repeat until all the children have
  joined the train.)*
(Begin slowing down.) **Chug-a-chug,
  chug-a-chug.**
(Slower) **Chug-a-chug, chug-a-
  chug. . . Chooo.**

Have children sit in a circle on the
floor.

3. Prayer Air!

(You'll need a Bible with a balloon
inside.)

Present the Bible with the balloon
inside. Say: **Do you like to have people tell you, "Thank you"? It makes
us feel good because we have done
something nice. God loves to hear
us tell him "thank you" for the good
things he does for us. Let's sing a
special thank you song to God.**

Lead children in singing the "Thank
You Song" several times.

Thank You Song

(Sing to the tune of "Row, Row,
Row Your Boat.")
**Thank you, thank you, thank you,
  God.**
Thank you from my heart.
**Thank you, thank you, thank you,
  God.**
Thank you from my heart.

Now have children sing the "Where,
When, What? Song."

Where, When, What? Song

(Sing to the tune of "Three Blind
Mice.")
Where do we pray?
Right here, anywhere!
When do we pray?
Right now, anytime!

What do we pray about?
All things without a doubt!
That's how we all can pray to God,
So let's pray now.

Open the Bible to Psalm 9. Remove
the balloon from the Bible and say:
**God has done many wonderful
things for us. We drew pictures of
some of those things right here on
our thank you note to God. Let's
pray and thank him for all those
things.**

Pray: **Thank you, God, for all the
wonderful things you've given us
and for sending Jesus to die for our
sins.**

As you blow up the balloon, go
around the circle having each child
thank God for one thing for every
breath you blow into the balloon.

Then say: **Because God is right
here with us, he has already heard
all our thank yous. So let's all cheer
for God as I let go of this balloon.**
Let go of the balloon and lead children in cheering.

4. Color Prayers

(You'll need different-colored
crayons.)

Gather the children together in
groups of three. Give each group a
different-colored crayon. Tell each
group to think of something that is the
color of the crayon that they can
thank God for, such as green grass or
blue sky. If kids quickly come up with
one thing, encourage them to think of
more. Give them a minute or less to
work together, then call on the groups
to share what they came up with.

5. Hannah Was Happy

(You'll need a Bible)

Open the Bible to 1 Samuel 1. Say:
I want to tell you thank you for

coming to class today. It makes me happy to see you here. Thank you for being good listeners when we have our story. Today's story is about a woman named Hannah. She wanted to have a baby. She went to church and prayed very hard. She was asking God to give her a baby. Ask:

● **What prayers does God hear?**
● **Why does God give us what we need?**
● **What do you think God did for Hannah?**
● **What do you think Hannah said?**

Say: **Hannah was so happy that she thanked and thanked God. When Hannah's little boy got big enough, she took him to the Temple where he could learn more about God and serve God. Hannah thanked God for giving her a baby. God gives us lots of good things, and it makes him happy when we tell him thank you.**

6. Thank You Balloons

(You'll need photocopies of the "Thank You Prayers" handout on page 54 and crayons.)

Give each child a copy of the "Thank You Prayers" handout. Have children color the children on the page, but not the balloons.

Then say: **Now let's pray a prayer of thanks to God and color one of the balloons.**

Help each child thank God for something such as parents or a nice day. Compliment each one for his or her prayer by saying: (Name), **God is pleased when you thank him like that.** Then have each child color one

balloon on the picture.

Say: **Take this "Thank You, God" page home and put it on your refrigerator. When you tell God "thank you," color another balloon.**

7. Flowers of Thanks

(You'll need English muffins, bananas, celery sticks, jelly, and spoons. Assemble a sample of the flower treat to show children.)

Give each child half of an English muffin, several slices of banana, and a celery stick. Show a sample of the flower treat. When children have assembled their own, let them each put a spoonful of jelly in the center of the muffin.

Say: **Giving people flowers is a nice way to say thank you. Let's thank God for our flower treats before we eat them. Say this prayer with me.** (Have children repeat the prayer after you, one line at a time.)

Dear God,
Roses are red.
Violets are blue.
I am so happy.
I want to thank you!

THANK YOU PRAYERS

Color a balloon whenever you tell God thank you.

Give It All You've Got

Preschoolers are usually not too joyful about giving away things that belong to them. But they can learn joyful giving through positive experiences—by having an opportunity to see how their gifts affect others. Use this lesson to show children how God uses them to help others.

A POWERFUL POINT

" 'Bring to the storehouse a full tenth of what you earn so there will be food in my house. Test me in this,' says the Lord All-Powerful. 'I will open the windows of heaven for you and pour out all the blessings you need' " (Malachi 3:10).

Children will learn:

We can feel good when we give to others.

A LOOK AT THE LESSON

1. Clean Up (10 minutes)
2. Prayer Train (5 minutes)
3. Prayer Air! (5 to 10 minutes)
4. You Choose (5 to 10 minutes)
5. Cheerful Giving (5 minutes)
6. Give a Gift (5 to 10 minutes)
7. Muffin Break (5 to 10 minutes)

THE FUN-TO-LEARN LESSON

1. Clean Up

(You'll need a variety of cleaning supplies.)

As children arrive tell them they'll be helping to clean up their classroom. Offer them a variety of things to do—clean the tables with shaving cream, wash the windows, wash and dry dishes, and sweep the floor.

Encourage children to work together and share the supplies. Praise them for the great job they're doing to clean up the room. When they're finished, gather the supplies and personally thank each child for the job he or she did.

2. Prayer Train

Gather the children together with the "Prayer-Train Rhyme." As you chug through the room, compliment children for cleaning it up so well.

Prayer-Train Rhyme

All aboard the prayer train!
(Start slowly.) **Chug-a-chug, chug-a-chug.**
(Faster) **Chug-a-chug, chug-a-chug.**
Chug-a-chug-a-choo-choo.
Jesus loves you!
Chug-a-chug-a-chee-chee.
Jesus loves me!
Up and down, up and down.
Jesus' love is all around!
(Repeat until all the children have joined the train.)
(Begin slowing down.) **Chug-a-chug, chug-a-chug.**
(Slower) **Chug-a-chug, chug-a-chug...Chooo.**

Have children sit on the floor.

3. Prayer Air!

(You'll need a Bible with a balloon in it.)

Show kids the Bible. Say: **It's good to pray before we read the Bible. When we pray we can ask God to help us understand the Bible. Let's sing our song about prayer.**

Where, When, What? Song

(Sing to the tune of "Three Blind Mice.")
Where do we pray?
Right here, anywhere!
When do we pray?
Right now, anytime!

What do we pray about?
All things without a doubt!
That's how we all can pray to God,
So let's pray now.

Open the Bible to Malachi 3. Remove the balloon from the Bible and say: **God gives us lots of good things, and he wants us to share what we have with other people. We can feel good when we give to others. God promises to be especially good to us when we do nice things for other people.**

Pray: **Thank you, God, for giving us good things. Help us to be joyful in giving things to other people. Amen.**

Say: **Let's pretend to put all kinds of good things in this balloon. As I blow up the balloon, you say what kinds of good things we can give or do for other people.**

Help children come up with things like being kind to their sister, giving a friend some candy, letting their brother play with a special toy.

When the balloon is full, say: **Now I can let go of this balloon and spread all those good things around the room to all of us!** Let go of the balloon.

4. You Choose

(You'll need pennies and three jars with pictures taped on them.)

Say: **One way we give nice things to people is by doing nice things for them. You gave me and other people in our church something nice when you cleaned up our room.**

Another way we keep our church looking good through our giving is by giving money to our church. Have you ever wondered what is done with money you put in the offering? I would like to show you what happens to it.

Bring out three jars with pictures taped on them: one showing the church staff, one showing missionaries, and one showing the building. Explain what the church does with the money given in each of those three areas. You might want to have a pastor or other church leader come and give those explanations. Set the jars on the floor.

Say: **I'm going to give some money to help our church, but I want you to help me. When I give you a penny, I would like you to decide where you would like the money to go to help our church. You may take the money and put it into any jar you want.**

One at a time, give each child a penny. Be sure and thank the children as they drop the money into the jars. If you have time, and care to give out more pennies, do two or three more rounds, letting children drop pennies into different jars. Be sure no pennies get into children's mouths.

5. Cheerful Giving

(Before class, photocopy the "Bible Puppets" handout on page 58. Cut the puppets out and color them. Glue them to craft sticks and insert them in a Bible.)

Have children sit in a circle on the

floor. Show them the Bible and open it to Acts 4:32-37. Remove the Bible puppets and go through the following script.

Puppet Script

Peter: Hi, boys and girls. My name is Peter. I want to tell you about the church I went to. I knew Jesus before he died on the cross for us, and I helped get the first church started. The whole group of us worked together to help each other. Here come some of my friends now. I wonder what they might need.

Couple: Hi, Peter. We were wondering if we could get some food from someone. We could share some of our firewood.

Peter: That would be just fine. I'll bring some food to your house, and you can give me some wood.

Group: Hi, Peter. We have some land we would like to sell so that we can use the money to help the family where the dad got hurt and can't work.

Peter: I think that sounds wonderful! Sharing what we have to help each other is what God wants us to do.

Put the puppets back in the Bible. Say: **God tells us in the Bible about good things people did long ago to help us know what we can be doing in our church. You did a good job working together and helping each other to take care of our church today. It makes us happy when we do good things for other people.**

6. Give a Gift

(You'll need berry baskets, chenille wire, doilies, crayons, and flowers.)

Give each child a berry basket, che-nille wire, and a paper doily. Have children color the doilies. Help each one attach the wire to the basket for a handle. Put the doilies in the baskets and let children choose a few cut flowers to put in their baskets.

Say: **Baskets of flowers are a nice gift. And it makes us feel good when we do something nice like that. Choose who you would like to give your basket to. It can be your mom or dad or a friend. Tell me who will get your special gift today.**

7. Muffin Break

(Before class, put muffins in a paper bag. Get the puppet of Peter out of the Bible.)

Have the children line up. Say: **Let's pretend we're like our Bible puppet friends. You can come up and ask Peter for some food. I think he has something special for you in this bag. But first, let's thank God for the food and for the nice things that people do for us.**

Say a brief prayer. Have the puppet thank the children for working in the church as you hand them each a muffin.

BIBLE PUPPETS

Don't Be Mad

When preschoolers are hurt or wronged by someone, they tend to react with anger. Forgiveness is not often a natural reaction. But Jesus knows all about anger and forgiveness. We can help our preschoolers begin to control their anger and be more forgiving by reminding them of how God has forgiven others.

Use this lesson to teach children they are able to forgive others.

A POWERFUL POINT

"If you forgive others for their sins, your Father in heaven will also forgive you for your sins" (Matthew 6:14).

Children will learn:

Jesus will help us forgive other people.

A LOOK AT THE LESSON

1. Chalk It Out (5 to 10 minutes)
2. Prayer Train (5 minutes)
3. Erase It (5 minutes)
4. Pop! Goes the Prayer Air (5 to 10 minutes)
5. Color My World With Love (10 minutes)
6. Families Forgive (5 minutes)
7. Bowl of Cherries (10 minutes)

THE FUN-TO-LEARN LESSON

1. Chalk It Out

(You'll need a chalkboard, chalk, and eraser.)

Greet children with chalk to draw on the chalkboard. Say: **Today we'll be learning about forgiving people who haven't been nice to us. That means we don't stay mad at them.** Ask:

● **How do you feel when someone takes a toy away from you?**

Say: **Jesus wants you to get rid of those unhappy feelings. And he can help us do that.**

Have each child draw an angry face on the chalkboard. Then have children erase the angry faces.

Say: **God wants to help us so we don't stay mad at people.**

2. Prayer Train

Gather the children together with the "Prayer-Train Rhyme."

Prayer-Train Rhyme

All aboard the prayer train!
(*Start slowly.*) **Chug-a-chug, chug-a-chug.**
(*Faster*) **Chug-a-chug, chug-a-chug.**
Chug-a-chug-a-choo-choo.
Jesus loves you!
Chug-a-chug-a-chee-chee.
Jesus loves me!
Up and down, up and down.
Jesus' love is all around!
(*Repeat until all the children have joined the train.*)
(*Begin slowing down.*) **Chug-a-chug, chug-a-chug.**
(*Slower*) **Chug-a-chug, chug-a-chug...Chooo.**

Seat children in a circle on the floor.

3. Erase It

(You'll need a chalkboard, chalk, and eraser.)

Show the children the clean chalkboard. Draw an angry face on it. Ask:

● **Do you feel this way sometimes?** Let children respond.

Say: **Jesus asked us to forgive people who do bad things to us. That means we shouldn't stay mad. Jesus forgives us for the wrong things we do. He knows how we feel. He can help us get over being mad if we ask him to.**

Erase the picture and ask:

● **What kind of face should we draw to show how we feel when we forgive someone?**

Draw a happy face on the chalkboard. Say: **God can help us get rid of all those bad feelings, just like I could erase that angry face that was on the chalkboard. Don't you like this picture better?**

Show me your smiles. You all have such nice smiles! God likes to see those smiles, too!

4. Pop! Goes the Prayer Air

(Before class, use a black marker to draw an angry face on a balloon. You'll need a Bible with a balloon in it and a pin.)

Present the Bible with the prayer balloon inside.

Say: **Let's ask God to help us when we're mad. Let's put all our angry feelings in this balloon. Who can tell me something you've been mad about?**

Inflate the balloon as children respond. Let them see the angry face grow as the balloon fills with air.

Say: **Watch what we can do with all these angry feelings.** Pop the balloon with the pin. **The angry feelings are gone! We don't have to stay mad**

at people. Jesus says we can forgive them and forget about it.

5. Color My World With Love

(You'll need paper, pencils, paint, paint shirts, paintbrushes, and markers or stickers.)

Give the children paper and pencils. Have them draw an angry face on their paper. Then give them paint shirts, paintbrushes, and thick yellow poster paint. Let them paint over their pictures.

Say: **Look, it's gone forever! You can never see that picture again. That's like what happens when we forgive someone. We get rid of the angry feelings. And Jesus will help us forgive others just like he forgives us.**

Assure children they can forgive and forget their angry feelings when they ask Jesus to help them.

When the paint dries, have children draw a happy picture over the paint or put stickers on the page.

6. Families Forgive

(You'll need a Bible.)
Ask:

● **How many of you have brothers or sisters?**

● **Do you ever get mad at them?**

Open the Bible to Genesis 27. Say: **Our Bible story today is about two brothers named Esau and Jacob. They fought all the time. Their mom and dad spent a lot of time trying to help them get along better. One day they had such a big fight that Jacob had to run away from home. He was gone a long time. He got very lonely for his family.**

Jacob was sorry about the big fight with his brother, and he decided he would go home and ask Esau to forgive the wrong things he had done.

Esau heard that Jacob was coming home. He missed his brother, and he didn't stay mad at him. He was glad Jacob was coming back. He ran out to meet him, and they hugged and forgave each other.

Jesus wants us to get along with our families. He wants to help us forgive each other just like he helped Jacob and Esau.

7. Bowl of Cherries

(Before class, empty a can of unsweetened tart red pie cherries in one bowl and a jar of maraschino cherries in another bowl.)

Offer one of each kind to the children. As they eat them say: **Both of these are cherries, but one is sweet and one is sour. We can choose to eat just the sweet ones. We can also choose to be mad or happy. Jesus will help us forgive each other. Let's not be like this sour cherry. Let's be like the sweet cherries and forgive others like Jesus forgave us.**

Give children sweet cherries and grapes or another fresh fruit for a treat.

Friendly Fellowship

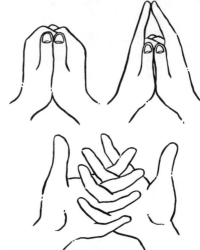

To a preschooler, church means learning about Jesus. Although they are just starting to learn the concept of relationships, preschoolers can begin to develop a concept of the church as people and friends. Use this lesson to promote friendships among the children.

A POWERFUL POINT

"The church everywhere in Judea, Galilee, and Samaria had a time of peace and became stronger. Respecting the Lord by the way they lived, and being encouraged by the Holy Spirit, the group of believers continued to grow" (Acts 9:31).

Children will learn:
Our church friends are important.

A LOOK AT THE LESSON

1. We Are the Church (5 minutes)
2. Prayer Train (5 minutes)
3. Stand Together (10 minutes)
4. Sent With Love (5 minutes)
5. Musical Parts (5 to 10 minutes)
6. We Are the Church (10 minutes)
7. Food Fellowship (10 minutes)

THE FUN-TO-LEARN LESSON

1. We Are the Church

Show children the finger play that uses this rhyme.
Here's the church.
Here's the steeple.
Open the door and see all the people!

Say: **The church is not just a building. The church is really made up of all the people that come to the church building to worship God.**

Help children do the finger play themselves. Say: **The church is made up of people who care about each other. Our church friends are important to us.**

2. Prayer Train

Gather children on the prayer train. As you chug around the room encourage the children to say the rhyme with you.

Prayer-Train Rhyme

All aboard the prayer train!
(Start slowly.) **Chug-a-chug, chug-a-chug.**

(Faster) **Chug-a-chug, chug-a-chug.**
Chug-a-chug-a-choo-choo.
Jesus loves you!
Chug-a-chug-a-chee-chee.
Jesus loves me!
Up and down, up and down.
Jesus' love is all around!
(Repeat until all the children have joined the train.)
(Begin slowing down.) **Chug-a-chug, chug-a-chug.**
(Slower) **Chug-a-chug, chug-a-chug . . . Chooo.**

Have children sit on the floor.

3. Stand Together

(You'll need several balls and a Bible with a balloon in it.)

Say: **Our church is an important part of our lives. Our friends are there. Going to church means we get to be with them. You're with friends right now. Let's do some fun things together as friends. As I tell you things, you can do them together.**

Have children form pairs. Give kids a few seconds between each of the following commands. Say:

Shake your hands up in the air.
Shake hands with each other.
Sit down and roll a ball back and forth between you.
Make funny faces at each other.
Stand up and do a high five.

Say: **We can do all kinds of fun things as friends together in the church, including learning from the Bible and praying together.**

Gather children in a circle on the floor. Open the Bible to Acts 9 and show it to the children.

Say: **The Bible tells us that people in the earliest churches worked together and were encouraged by God. They were good friends. And** they spent time worshiping and praying together. Let's sing our song about prayer.

Where, When, What? Song

(Sing to the tune of "Three Blind Mice.")
Where do we pray?
Right here, anywhere!
When do we pray?
Right now, anytime!

What do we pray about?
All things without a doubt!
That's how we all can pray to God,
So let's pray now.

Get the balloon out of the Bible. Ask:

● **Who would like to say a prayer to thank God for our friends in the church?**

Blow air in the balloon as children pray. Then release the balloon and let it fly through the air as you say together: **Thank you, God, for friends!**

Have children get back with their partners and sit on the floor. Say: **Let's finish our time with our partners by turning around so our backs are together. Lock your arms with your partner's and push against each other to see if you can stand up together, back to back.**

Help children get their arms locked together and let them help themselves up. If some have trouble, let them turn around and help each other up.

Say: **You did such a good job helping each other up! That's how we help other people. Our church friends can help us when we need help, just like we helped each other get up. Our church friends are important to us. We can help each other when we need help.**

4. Sent With Love

(You'll need a Bible.)

Have children return to a circle on the floor. Open the Bible to Acts 13:1-4. Ask:

● **Have you ever moved to a different town?**

● **Did you go to a new church there?**

Say: **Today our story is about Paul and Barnabas. They were good friends who went to the same church. One day while they were praying God told them to move to a different town and start a new church.**

Paul and Barnabas asked their friends to pray with them. Everyone in the church got together and prayed and asked God to help Paul and Barnabas. The friends knew they would miss Paul and Barnabas, but they also knew God would help them start a new church.

Paul and Barnabas had good friends in the church who were important to them. Our church friends are important to us, too.

5. Musical Parts

(You'll need a cassette tape and recorder.)

Say: **We can all have a part in our church. We're going to pretend we are different musical instruments and play a song together.** Divide the class into three sections: drums, horns, and violins.

Tell the drum section: **When the music plays, you say, "Boom boom" and then thump on the floor with your hand.**

Tell the horn section: **When the music plays, you say, "Toot toot," with your hands around your mouth.**

Tell the violin section: **When the music plays, show me how you would play a violin and hum the tune.**

Turn on a familiar music tape or sing a favorite song and let the children try their parts. Use a couple of short songs if you have time.

Then say: **Isn't it fun to work and play together with our friends in the church? Our church friends are important to us.**

6. We Are the Church

(Before class, cut out several copies of the "Church and God's People" handout on page 66. You'll also need copies of the "Dot-to-Dot Church" handout on page 67, crayons, scissors, and glue.)

Show the church pictures to the children. Tell children what each person does. Say: **We can have different jobs to do and work together in our church. I want you to choose what you would like to do in the church.**

Let each child choose a picture.

Say: **All these jobs are very important. God has a special job in the church for each of us. Let's make the church so we can put these people inside of it.**

Give each child a photocopy of the "Dot-to-Dot Church" handout. Help children fill in the lines and color their churches. Cut open the doors for them. Turn the page over and glue in the square each child chose so that the picture shows when the doors are opened. Let children open and close the doors.

Say: **Each of these people in the church is important to us. They're all our friends.**

7. Food Fellowship

(You'll need peanut butter, jelly, bread, plastic knives, and plates.)

Form groups of four. Have children work together in their groups at a table to make peanut butter and jelly sandwiches. In front of one child place some peanut butter; in front of another, some jelly; in front of the third, a slice of bread on a plate; and in front of the fourth, a plastic knife.

Tell children to work together sharing what they have in front of them to make sandwiches. Give helpful suggestions on how to work together. When each group is ready, place a second slice of bread on top, cut the sandwich into fourths, and let kids share it.

Say: **We worked together with our friends to make our peanut butter and jelly treats. Our friends in the church are important to us, and God is pleased when we all work together.**

THE CHURCH AND GOD'S PEOPLE

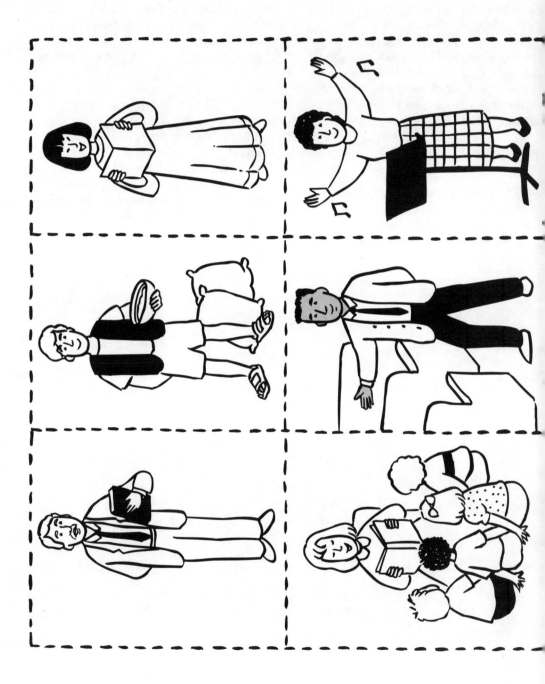

DOT-TO-DOT CHURCH

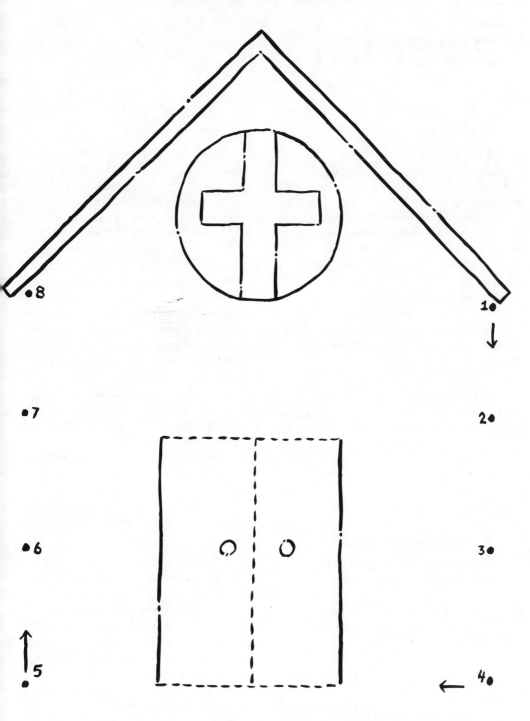

God Made Us Special

As preschoolers become more and more aware of their world, they begin to realize that some people look differently, talk differently, and even act differently from them. It can frighten preschoolers and cause them to reject or make fun of others. Children need to realize that God has made our entire world, including lots of different kinds of people. Use this lesson to help children accept people the way they are and realize God has made us all for his special plan.

A POWERFUL POINT

"God has made us what we are. In Christ Jesus, God made us to do good works, which God planned in advance for us to live our lives doing" (Ephesians 2:10).

Children will learn:

God made us special and has a perfect plan for us.

A LOOK AT THE LESSON

1. Special Crosses (5 to 10 minutes)
2. Special Ways (5 minutes)
3. Animal Prayers (5 to 10 minutes)
4. You Are Special (5 minutes)
5. Together Colors (10 minutes)
6. Fruit Favorites (10 minutes)

THE FUN-TO-LEARN LESSON

1. Special Crosses

(You'll need the modeling dough.)
As children arrive, greet them and ask them to take a piece of modeling dough and make a cross. As children are making the crosses, wander from child to child, making positive comments about their creations. Display the completed crosses in front of the class.

When everyone has made a cross, gather children around the display.

Say: **You all have made crosses. The cross is a sign we use to show that we believe Jesus died on the cross for the wrong things we've done. He came to life again so we could live with him forever in heaven.**

Our crosses all mean the same thing but look at how differently they're made. Some are big and some small. Ask:

● **We can all love Jesus. But do we all look the same or act the same?** Let children respond.

Say: **We're learning today that God made us special because he loves us.**

2. Special Ways

(You'll need masking tape and Hershey's Kisses.)

Say: **There are a lot of people who love Jesus. But different people like to show him their love in their own special ways. Some people like to sing. Some people like to pray. Some people like to study the Bible. We all like to do those things when we're Christians, but we each may do them a little bit differently.**

Put a 4-foot long strip of wide

masking tape on the floor. Place a bowl of Hershey's Kisses on the floor at the end of the tape.

Say: **I want you to have a piece of candy. You can only get to the candy by following the piece of tape. But I want you to get to the candy by choosing your own special way. You can walk along the tape, crawl along the tape, hop along the tape, or find another way to follow the tape to the candy. I want you to decide which way would be the most fun for you.**

When all children have a piece of candy, say: **There's only one way to become a Christian. We all must believe in Jesus to be Christians. But we can tell God and show God we love him in our own special ways. In fact, God made each of us different and expects us to do things differently.**

3. Animal Prayers

(You'll need a Bible.)

Have children gather in a circle around you. Ask:

● **What kinds of things do you see at the zoo?**

● **What would you think if you went to the zoo, and there were only monkeys in all the cages?**

Say: **God made all different kinds of animals. We enjoy seeing all those animals at the zoo. God also made all different kinds of people. We can learn to enjoy all kinds of people. God made everyone special, and he has a plan for everyone.**

Sing the following prayer song together.

Where, When, What? Song

(Sing to the tune of "Three Blind Mice.")

Where do we pray?
Right here, anywhere!
When do we pray?

Right now, anytime!

What do we pray about?
All things without a doubt!
That's how we all can pray to God,
So let's pray now.

Present the Bible and open it to Ephesians 2. Say: **God made each of us just the way we are. Each of us is special, and God has a special plan for our lives. Let's celebrate how special God has made us.**

Lead children in prayer, thanking God for making each of us special. Encourage each child to pray and then say to each child: **Your prayer to God was very special, just like you're special.**

4. You Are Special

(You'll need a Bible, food pictures, and a napkin.)

Say: **Let's look at some things about us that are special. When I call out something about you, jump up. Then you can sit back down.**

Go through the questions, having the children respond by jumping up and sitting back down. If you have children in your class who would have trouble jumping up, just have children raise their hands. After every question, tell the standing children: **You are special because you** (fill in the trait from the question). For example, for the first question you would say, "You are special because you have long hair."

Ask:

● **Who has long hair?**
● **Who has short hair?**
● **Who has brown eyes?**
● **Who has blue eyes?**
● **Who has dark hair?**
● **Who has light hair?**
● **Who needs to sleep?**
● **Who has a brother?**
● **Who needs to breathe?**

● **Who needs to eat?**

● **Who can smile?**

Say: **We're different in many ways, but in some ways we're the same. God made each of us special in his plan.**

Before telling the story, wrap the pictures of food in the napkin and put it in the Bible at Acts 10:9-16.

Say: **Our Bible story today is about a man named Peter who didn't know if some people could be Christians because they didn't eat the same food he did. God showed Peter that what people ate wasn't as important as what Peter thought it was. Loving Jesus was much more important. Let me tell you what happened to Peter.**

Open the Bible and take out the napkin. Say: **While Peter was praying, he had a dream about food. Have any of you ever dreamed about food? In his dream he saw a huge sheet full of different kinds of food to eat. Some of what Peter saw was food that Peter didn't think Christians should eat.**

Open the napkin with the pictures of food. Hold up a few pictures and ask the children to raise their hands if they like to eat that food.

Say: **We don't all like to eat the same things. But we can still all love Jesus.**

In Peter's dream, God told him it was OK to eat different foods. God said the important thing is that everyone love Jesus. After that, Peter told many people about Jesus, even if they liked different foods.

We can be friends with all kinds of people, even if they do things differently from us.

5. Together Colors

(You'll need poster paints, paper, craft sticks, and paint shirts.)

Say: **God has made each of us special. He gives each of us special ideas and things we can do. When we put our special abilities together with other people's, we can make things better.**

What if there were only three colors in the world? We'd get tired of that. Show the kids red, yellow, and blue paint.

Say: **These are three different colors, but they can make more colors when we put them together. I will let you mix them and see.**

Give each child a sheet of white paper, a craft stick, and a paint shirt. Put some paint on their paper. Let them mix red and yellow to make orange. Then have kids mix yellow and blue to make green. Let them experiment with mixing any other colors.

Say: **See all the special colors we made? We made lots of different colors. God made lots of different people, and he made each one special. He made each of us able to do special things to serve him.**

6. Fruit Favorites

(You'll need cups, spoons, and fruit cocktail.)

Give each child a cup and a plastic spoon. Bring out the fruit cocktail. Say: **Raise your hand if you like peaches. Stomp your feet if you like pears. Clap your hands if you like grapes and cherries.**

Let's say a prayer and thank God he made all these different fruits for us to enjoy. Let's also thank God for making each person special.

Lead children in a prayer. Serve them fruit cocktail.

Part 4: Look What Happens When People Pray!

Daniel Gets Help

Children are always eager to hear stories of kings, lions, and victory for their heroes. Young children need heroes, and Daniel is a great hero for preschoolers to pattern their lives after. Daniel was a man of prayer, loyalty, and commitment. Use this lesson to teach children the importance of prayer.

A POWERFUL POINT

"Daniel's God is the living God; he lives forever. His kingdom will never be destroyed, and his rule will never end...He is the one who saved Daniel from the power of the lions" (Daniel 6:26-27).

Children will learn:
Prayer is very important.

A LOOK AT THE LESSON

1. Looking at Lions (5 minutes)
2. Roaring Around (2 to 3 minutes)
3. Prayer Train (5 to 7 minutes)
4. Prayer Power (5 to 7 minutes)
5. Looking Like Lions (10 minutes)
6. A Roaring Good Time (10 minutes)
7. Peanut Butter Lions (5 to 7 minutes)

THE FUN-TO-LEARN LESSON

1. Looking at Lions

(You'll need a copy of the "Lion" handout on page 76.)

Show children a copy of the "Lion" handout. Ask:
- **What kinds of teeth do lions have?**
- **What kind of paws do lions have?**
- **What kinds of claws do lions have?**
- **Have you ever been to the zoo and seen a real lion?**
- **Have you heard a lion roar?**
- **How did you feel being so close to a lion?**

Say: **Today we'll be hearing about a man named Daniel who spent the night in a cage with hungry lions.**

What do you think Daniel did in there most of the night? Daniel prayed and God made sure the lions didn't eat him. Prayer was very important to Daniel, and we're going to be learning how important it is to us, too.

2. Roaring Around

(You'll need the "Lion" handouts.)

Pass out copies of the "Lion" handout (p. 76) to children and say: **Let's pretend we're lions. Roar around our room like a lion.**

Give the children a couple of minutes to be lions. When you're ready to move on, thank the children for being such good lions.

3. Prayer Train

(You'll need a Bible.)

Bring the children together in a circle by gathering them on the prayer train.

Prayer-Train Rhyme

All aboard the prayer train!
(*Start slowly.*) **Chug-a-chug, chug-a-chug.**
(*Faster*) **Chug-a-chug, chug-a-chug.**
Chug-a-chug-a-choo-choo.
Jesus loves you!
Chug-a-chug-a-chee-chee.
Jesus loves me!
Up and down, up and down.
Jesus' love is all around!
(*Repeat until all the children have joined the train.*)
(*Begin slowing down.*) **Chug-a-chug, chug-a-chug.**
(*Slower*) **Chug-a-chug, chug-a-chug . . . Chooo.**

Present the Bible. Say: **Our Bible story teaches us about how important it is to pray. So let's sing our prayer song. Be thinking of an important prayer while we sing.**

Where, When, What? Song

(Sing to the tune of "Three Blind Mice.")
Where do we pray?
Right here, anywhere!
When do we pray?
Right now, anytime!

What do we pray about?
All things without a doubt!
That's how we all can pray to God,
So let's pray now.

Ask:

● **What important things have you thought of to pray about?**

After each child offers something to pray about, affirm that child by saying what a good thing that is to pray about.

Say: **Prayer is very important.**

Lead the children in praying about the things they mentioned.

4. Prayer Power

(You'll need a Bible.)

Gather the children in a circle on the floor. Turn to Daniel 6 in the Bible.

Say: **Our Bible story today is about a man named Daniel who was thrown into a cage with several lions, and he stayed there all night.** Ask:

● **Why do you think Daniel was thrown into the lions' cage?**

Say: **Listen carefully and I will tell you why he was thrown into the lions' cage. Daniel had been captured by soldiers and taken away to a strange country. He tried hard to be good and obey the people in this strange country. The people liked him very much. The king liked him so much he decided to give Daniel a special job. Some men heard that Daniel got the special job instead of them, and they got mad. Show me how you look when you're mad.**

The men wanted to get Daniel in trouble, but he wasn't doing anything wrong. They had to think up a plan. Scratch your heads and wrinkle your faces like you're thinking. Now put your hands around your ears so you can listen while I whisper what they planned to do.

Whisper: **Let's tell the king he's wonderful, and we think all the people should bow down and pray to him. He will like that. Let's get him to sign a paper that says that** anyone who won't do that will be thrown in the cage with the hungry lions!

Resume normal speaking and say: **And that's what the men did. They knew that Daniel would pray only to his God, and that Daniel would never pray to the king.**

Get on your knees and show me how Daniel might have bowed down and prayed to God. Let the children bow to the floor. **That is what Daniel did. He did that every day, three times a day. But he wouldn't bow down and pray to the king.**

When the king found out that Daniel wouldn't pray to him, he felt very bad. He liked Daniel, but he had signed the paper saying anyone who wouldn't pray to him would be thrown in the lions' cage, called a lions' "den."

So Daniel was put in the lion's cage because he refused to pray to anyone but God. Do you think God was in there with him? Yes, God is everywhere! Do you think Daniel bowed down and prayed to God while he was in that cage? Show me again how we bow and pray.

The king worried about Daniel all night. He hurried out the next morning to see if the lions had eaten Daniel. He yelled, "Daniel, are you alive?" Stand up, put your hands around your mouth and yell, "Daniel, are you alive?" Better yell once more, "Daniel, are you alive?" Give children a chance to listen.

Make your voice sound strong and say: **"Yes! I sure am alive!"** Daniel said. **"My great God has kept me safe from these lions all night long. They haven't opened their mouths."**

The king was so happy to hear that! He said "Wonderful! Get Daniel out of there right away, and we will all bow down and pray to his God."

Let's bow down right now and tell God how important prayer is to us. Say a brief prayer.

5. Looking Like Lions

(Before class, cut one side out of each paper bag. Use the cut-away piece to make curly strips of paper. You'll also need glue sticks and a mirror.)

Seat the children around the tables and give each child a brown paper bag, a glue stick, and several curled pieces of paper. Let children glue the curly strips on the top of the bag to make a lion mane. Have kids put the bags on their heads. Let them look in a mirror and growl.

Say: **Prayer was very important to Daniel. Because he prayed to God and not to the king, God saved him from the lions. Prayer is very important to us, too.**

6. A Roaring Good Time

(Before class, put wide masking tape on the floor in a square, 6 or more feet across. Put an X with the tape in the middle of the square.)

Play Daniel in the Lions' Den as you would Ring Around a Rosy, keeping all children inside the masking-tape square.

You may start in the center as Daniel, or choose a child to be Daniel. Let the other children put on their lion manes and prowl around inside the taped area. Encourage them to walk around Daniel and growl. Then have the class say:

Lions: Daniel in the lions' den.
Daniel in the lions' den.
Daniel: Pray! Pray!
All: They all fall down!

Have the lions fall down. Have the last one to fall take off his or her lion mane and go to the center of the cage as Daniel. Continue the game until all the children have been Daniel.

Ask: **How important is prayer?** Have them repeat after you: **Prayer is very important!**

7. Peanut Butter Lions

(You'll need animal crackers, craft sticks, and peanut butter.)

Give each child several animal crackers and a craft stick. Tell children to pick out the lion crackers and frost them with peanut butter. Then pray: **Thank you, God that we can pray. We know prayer is important. Help us to pray every day like Daniel did.**

Let children enjoy the crackers for a snack.

LION

Esther Gains Courage

Esther is a powerful story about people committed to prayer. Esther's response to her life-threatening problem was to call upon people to pray. The result is her acceptance of God's plan. Although God is never mentioned in the book, his perfect timing and protection is evident. Use this lesson to show children that God answers our prayers at just the right time. We can trust him.

A POWERFUL POINT

"Go and get all the Jewish people in Susa together. For my sake, give up eating; do not eat or drink for three days, night and day. I and my servant girls will also give up eating. Then I will go to the king, even though it is against the law, and if I die, I die" (Esther 4:16).

Children will learn:

God knows when to answer our prayers.

A LOOK AT THE LESSON

1. Kings and Queens (5 to 7 minutes)
2. Finger Queens (10 minutes)
3. Calendar Calamities (3 to 5 minutes)
4. Perfect Timing (10 to 12 minutes)
5. Time Is Running Out (5 to 10 minutes)
6. Timely Treats (10 minutes)

THE FUN-TO-LEARN LESSON

1. Kings and Queens

(Before class, make cardboard crowns and decorate a chair with a covering for a throne.)

Wear a crown as you greet the children. Say: **Today we're going to hear about a very brave queen.** Invite children to wear crowns and sit on the throne. Ask:

● **What do you think it would be like to be a king or a queen in a castle?**

Say: **Sometimes being a queen isn't easy. The queen in our story today had to pray for help and then do something very dangerous to save her people. But God knew just when to answer her prayer. We'll learn more about this queen in a little bit.**

2. Finger Queens

(Before class, cut several sheets of yellow construction paper into 1×2-inch strips. Trim one edge of the 2-inch side with pinking shears. You'll also need cupcake papers, crayons, a watercolor pen, and tape.)

Give each child a strip of yellow construction paper to use as a crown and a cupcake paper to be a dress. Have children color the cupcake papers and put them over their left index fingers. Help each child poke a hole in the middle of the cupcake paper and pull it down to the second knuckle. Put a piece of tape on one end of each yellow strip and let the child wrap it around the tip of the index finger and tape it in place. Use a watercolor pen to draw a face on each child's finger between the paper crown and the cupcake paper.

Let the children have a puppet show. Ask the following questions and let the children respond using their queen puppets:

● **What kinds of things might a queen say?**

● **What kinds of things might a queen pray about?**

Say: **The queen in our story today had to pray to save her people from a wicked enemy. But God answered her prayer. God knows when to answer our prayers.**

3. Calendar Calamities

(You'll need watches, clocks, a kitchen timer, and a calendar.)

Let children play with the watches and clocks. Talk about how important it is to learn to tell time. Show them the calendar. Ask:

● **Do you ever mark a calendar for a special day?**

● **When is your birthday?**

● **Do you mark it on your calendar?**

Say: **In our lesson today, we'll hear about a day that was marked on a calendar that would be a very bad day for a lot of people. The day was marked for them to be attacked by a wicked enemy. Queen Esther needed to find a way to change that. But before she did anything she took time to pray.**

Gather the children together with the "Prayer-Train Rhyme."

Prayer-Train Rhyme

All aboard the prayer train!
(Start slowly.) **Chug-a-chug, chug-a-chug.**
(Faster) **Chug-a-chug, chug-a-chug.**
Chug-a-chug-a-choo-choo.
Jesus loves you!
Chug-a-chug-a-chee-chee.
Jesus loves me!
Up and down, up and down.
Jesus' love is all around!
(Repeat until all the children have joined the train.)
(Begin slowing down.) **Chug-a-chug, chug-a-chug.**
(Slower) **Chug-a-chug, chug-a-chug...Chooo.**

Gather the children in a circle on the floor. Say: **Let's take time right now to pray and thank God that he answers our prayers.** Pray a brief prayer.

4. Perfect Timing

(You'll need a calendar and a black marker.)

Ask:

● **Have you ever been chosen to do something special? What was it?**

Say: **Esther was a young woman who lived with her Uncle Mordecai** (MORE-dee-kye). **They had been taken away from their homes to a different country. Many of their friends were taken, too. The king in that country was looking for a queen. He chose Esther to be his queen because she was very pretty and she was very kind. We had some very pretty queens on our fingers, didn't we?**

The king had a helper named Haman that didn't like Esther's Uncle Mordecai. He wanted to have him killed because Mordecai said God was more important than the king.

Raise your hand if you think God is more important than kings. Clap your hands if you think God is more important than queens. Stand up and cheer if you think God is more important than anything!

Give children time to respond, then say: **The king liked Mordecai, so Haman wanted to find a way to trick the king into killing Mordecai. He told the king there were a lot of people from another country that didn't like him. Haman said they should all be killed. He had the king sign a paper saying that on a certain day all the people from that country would be killed. Those people included Mordecai's family and friends.**

Show children the calendar. Mark a day on it with a black marker and say: **Esther wanted to save her family and friends! What could she do? The people from Esther's country began to pray as hard as they could. They prayed God wouldn't let them be killed. They prayed for Esther, because she was the queen and Mordecai said it was her job to talk to the king. Esther took three days to pray, and she waited for** God **to tell her what to do. She knew she had to tell the king the truth about his nasty helper, Haman. But it was against the law for anyone to go to the king without being asked. Even the queen wasn't supposed to do that. Esther was scared, but she believed God would help her talk to the king.**

Ask:

● **Have you ever been afraid to talk to someone? Show me a scared look.**

● **Did you know God would be with you to help you? Show me how you look when God helps you.**

Say: **When Queen Esther told the king the truth, he got so mad at Haman that he had him killed right away! And the king said the people from Esther's country could fight back when the day came that people would try to kill them. God had provided a way to save the people, but they had to wait until that day to see what would happen.**

Mark off the days on the calendar right up to the square marked in black. Have the children count them with you.

Say: **God knows the right time to answer our prayers. He gave Esther and her people courage to fight for themselves. So when the time came, the people from Esther's country were ready to win the battle and they did. God answered their prayers at just the right time.**

Ask:

● **What did Esther do to help save her people?**

● **When did God answer Esther's prayer?**

Say: **God knows what's best for us, and he answers our prayers at just the right time. Sometimes we don't know what's going on, but God always does.**

5. Time Is Running Out

(You'll need a kitchen timer.)

When you're finished with the story, ring the kitchen timer to get the children's attention.

Say: **Let's play a game about taking time out to pray. You can all walk around the room until you hear the timer. Then I want you to freeze in place. We can say, "God knows when to answer our prayers." Then you can walk again until you hear the timer.**

Let the children walk around for about 10 seconds, then ring the timer. Lead the children in saying: **God knows when to answer our prayers.** Then start kids walking again. Stop them with the timer three or four more times, repeating the sentence together each time.

Afterward, say: **You didn't know when the timer would go off. None of us knows when God is going to answer prayers, except that he always answers them at just the right time.**

6. Timely Treats

(You'll need bagels, cream cheese, raisins, and carrot sticks.)

Gather children at a table. Give each child a half of a bagel. Let children frost their bagels with flavored cream cheese. Have children arrange their raisins on their bagels like numbers on a clock and use the carrot sticks to look like hands on a clock. Ask children what time their clocks say it is.

Say: **Whatever time it is, God knows just the right time to answer our prayers. Right now it's time to have something to eat.**

Have children pray this treat-time prayer together:

Now it's time to have my treat. Thank you, God, for food to eat.

Gideon Finds Faith

Gideon's story tells of a reluctant leader who had his fears and doubts. However, Gideon's response to his human weakness is commendable. He humbly pursued God in prayer, and God helped him overcome his fears. Preschoolers often deal with fear and need continual demonstrations of love. Use this lesson to teach the children everyone has fears, and that God understands and helps us overcome our fears.

A POWERFUL POINT

"Then Gideon said to God, 'Don't be angry with me if I ask just one more thing. Please let me make one more test. Let only the wool be dry while the ground around it gets wet with dew.' That night God did that very thing. Just the wool was dry, but the ground around it was wet with dew" (Judges 6:39).

Children will learn:

God will help us when we get scared.

A LOOK AT THE LESSON

1. Who's Afraid? (5 minutes)
2. Rainy-Day Fun (10 minutes)
3. Prayer Train (5 to 7 minutes)
4. Doubts and Dew Drops (5 to 7 minutes)
5. Hats Off to Gideon (10 minutes)
6. Wet Wool (5 to 7 minutes)
7. Fun Hats (5 to 7 minutes)

THE FUN-TO-LEARN LESSON

1. Who's Afraid?

Say: **How many of you have ever been afraid? The Bible teaches us that God understands our fears, and he is there to help us with them. Have you ever been afraid of the dark, or someone's dog, or a loud noise?** Don't get kids telling scary stories, but give them an opportunity to tell about a time they were afraid. Focus on God's ability to help them be brave.

Then say: **God will help us when we're scared. He's always with us, and he wants us to ask him for help when we get frightened.**

Form pairs. Have partners tell each other, "You don't ever need to be scared because God is with you."

2. Rainy-Day Fun

(You'll need an umbrella, a tablecloth, two colors of construction paper cut in 5-inch squares, and a squirt bottle of water.)

Get out the umbrella and hold it over your head. Say: **Today we're going to hear about a man named Gideon who asked God to make something wet in one place.**

Have the tablecloth laid out on the floor with the colored pieces of construction paper placed in the center in checkerboard fashion.

Have a child use the squirt bottle to try to squirt the water onto only one color of paper. The child with the squirt bottle must stand off the tablecloth. Give the other children a turn also.

Say: **It's hard to make just one spot wet. But God did that for Gideon. Gideon was scared, so he prayed for a sign that God was really with him. God answered Gideon's prayer by making only the one spot wet.**

3. Prayer Train

Collect the children in a circle with your prayer train.

Prayer-Train Rhyme

All aboard the prayer train!
(Start slowly.) **Chug-a-chug, chug-a-chug.**
(Faster) **Chug-a-chug, chug-a-chug. Chug-a-chug-a-choo-choo. Jesus loves you! Chug-a-chug-a-chee-chee. Jesus loves me! Up and down, up and down. Jesus' love is all around!**
(Repeat until all the children have joined the train.)
(Begin slowing down.) **Chug-a-chug, chug-a-chug.**
(Slower) **Chug-a-chug, chug-a-chug . . . Chooo.**

Have everyone sit down in the circle.

4. Doubts and Dew Drops

Say: **Have you ever gotten up early in the morning and found the ground outside wet even though it hadn't rained? That kind of water on the grass is called dew. It comes out of the ground and makes the grass wet.**

Today our story is about a soldier named Gideon who was afraid because he wasn't sure God was with him. An angel told him that God would help him, but he was still worried. We can always be sure that God will help us if we ask him for help when we're frightened.

5. Hats Off to Gideon

(You'll need paper bowls, foil, a hole punch, chenille wire, stickers, and a mirror.)

Say: **Let's make soldier hats so we can join Gideon's army and find out what God did to make him brave.**

Give each child a paper bowl and a square of foil. Have children wrap the foil around the bowl, pressing it to the form of the bowl. With the hole punch, make two holes across from each other near the top of the bowl.

Give each child two 12-inch pieces of chenille wire to put through the holes and twist the ends closed. Have children decorate their foil hats with stickers. Let children put their hats on, twist the chenille wires together under their chins, and look at themselves in the mirror.

Say: **We don't have to worry about getting scared because God will help us, just like army hats help protect people's heads when they are in the army. God will help us if we pray to him. Let's sing our prayer song right now.**

Where, When, What? Song

(Sing to the tune of "Three Blind Mice.")
**Where do we pray?
Right here, anywhere!
When do we pray?
Right now, anytime!**

**What do we pray about?
All things without a doubt!
That's how we all can pray to God,
So let's pray now.**

Lead your kids in praying to thank God for being ready to help us when we get scared.

6. Wet Wool

(You'll need a Bible, soldier hats, and two pieces of wool fleece.)

When children have all made soldier hats, have them wear their hats and march around the room. Say: **Let's march off to join Gideon's army and be brave soldiers for God.**

Gather the children in a circle on the floor. Let them keep their hats on.

Open the Bible to Judges 6 and show it to the children. Place a piece of fleece in front of you and say: **Gideon was so worried because his army was small and the other country had a very big army. Show me how he must have looked when he was worried.** Wring your hands and join the children in their expressions of worry.

Gideon needed to know that God was with him before he could get
over his fear. **This is a piece of wool from a sheep. One night Gideon took a piece of wool like this and put it on the ground and asked God to make just the wool wet and not the ground. He said, "If there is water only on the wool and not on the ground, then I will know that you will keep me safe." Gideon went to bed. He was trusting God to give him an answer in the morning. Let's lie down and go to bed with Gideon. Close your eyes. No peeking!**

After about five seconds of silence, say: **Wake up, kids! It's time to see if God did what Gideon asked him to do. You know what, the fleece was wet!** Take the squirt bottle, wet the fleece, and then let the children feel it. Say: **Yes, God answered Gideon's prayer. He felt better, but before the day was over, his fear was coming back. Use your fingers and have them creep up from your toes to your chin. I think that's the way fear came back to Gideon. Do you know what Gideon did? He went back to God and prayed some more. Do you think it's OK to ask God to help us again if we still have a problem? Raise your hands high in the air if you think it's OK. Now sit real still and listen to what Gideon did the second time.**

Remove the wet piece of wool and place a second piece of wool on the floor in front of you. **Listen closely to Gideon's second prayer. "Dear God, please don't be angry with me if I ask just one more thing. Please let me make one more test. Tomorrow morning let the wool be dry while the ground around it gets wet. Then I'll really know you are with me, God." When Gideon went to bed that night he believed God would answer him. Let's go to sleep again and see**

if God was patient with Gideon. Let's see if God answered his prayer.

Have children lie down and close their eyes. After about five seconds say: **Wake up and feel the wool. It was still dry!** Spray water on the floor around the wool as you say: **But you know what? The ground around the fleece was wet! God answered Gideon's prayer, and Gideon knew God would be with him. Gideon won that war and many others for God. God understands when we are scared.** Ask:

● **What should we do when we get scared?**

Say: **We can always know that God will help us when we ask for his help. When we get frightened, he is always there to help us.**

7. Fun Hats

(Children will need their soldier hats and napkins. You'll need an umbrella and a box of cereal.)

Have children take off their soldier hats, set them on the table, and put napkins inside. Say this treat-time prayer together: **Now it's time to have my treat. Thank you, God, for food to eat.**

Open your umbrella, turn it upside down, and empty a box of dry cereal (maybe Cap'n Crunch) into it. Say: **Let's pretend you're the captain of an army and you're having a party because you know that God helps you when you're scared.** Let the children reach into your umbrella and get two handfuls of cereal to put in their soldier hats. Enjoy the snack together.

Samson Regains Strength

Preschoolers know what it's like to want to be big and strong. Like Samson, children may have a tendency to misuse the strength they already have. They need to learn that God is loving and forgiving, but that he is disappointed by the wrong things we do. Use this lesson to teach the children that God will strengthen us so we can help others.

A POWERFUL POINT

"Then Samson prayed to the Lord, 'Lord God, remember me. God, please give me strength one more time so I can pay these Philistines back for putting out my two eyes!' " (Judges 16:28).

Children will learn:

Our strength comes from God.

A LOOK AT THE LESSON

1. Stronger Than Steel (10 minutes)
2. Prayer Train (5 to 7 minutes)
3. Breakaway Buddies (5 minutes)
4. Samson's Secret (5 to 7 minutes)
5. Haircuts (7 to 10 minutes)
6. Strong Treats (10 minutes)

THE FUN-TO-LEARN LESSON

1. Stronger Than Steel

(Before class, tie an inflated balloon to each end of a cardboard tube. Cover the tube with silver duct tape to complete your pretend barbells. Fill a metal box with heavy items and tape it shut with duct tape.)

Greet children and show them the pretend barbells and heavy metal box.

Say: **Today we're going to learn about a man who was very strong. His name was Samson.**

This box is heavy and very strong. You can kick it, hit it, and stand on it, but you can't hurt it a bit. It's so heavy you probably can't lift it. But Samson could have crushed it with his bare hands. God gave him a special gift of strength. But Samson didn't always act the way he should.

Let the children play with the box. Show children the barbells. Say: **Let's pretend these are real barbells. If they were, we probably couldn't lift them. Real barbells are something people lift to help them become strong. You can pretend you're real strong and lift these up over your head.**

You can show me how strong you are by playing a game with me.

Sit down at a table and let the children arm wrestle with you. Let them win.

Say: **God gave Samson incredible strength. And God will give us strength. He will give us all the strength we need to do whatever he wants us to do.**

2. Prayer Train

(You'll need a Bible.)

Gather the children around you with the prayer train.

Prayer-Train Rhyme

All aboard the prayer train!
(Start slowly.) **Chug-a-chug, chug-a-chug.**
(Faster) **Chug-a-chug, chug-a-chug. Chug-a-chug-a-choo-choo.**
Jesus loves you!
Chug-a-chug-a-chee-chee.
Jesus loves me!
Up and down, up and down.
Jesus' love is all around!
(Repeat until all the children have joined the train.)
(Begin slowing down.) **Chug-a-chug, chug-a-chug.**
(Slower) **Chug-a-chug, chug-a-chug...Chooo.**

Have children sit in a circle on the floor. Present the Bible and ask:

● **Who is the strongest person you know?**

● **Do you think our Bible tells us anything about being strong?**

Say: **Yes, it tells us a lot of things about being strong and helping other people. Today we're learning about Samson. God made him very strong, but Samson didn't always act the way he should. So God took his strength away from him. Samson forgot we get our strength from God. Stand up and show me the muscles in your arms.**

Have children flex their muscles. As children do the following exercises, go around and encourage and affirm them for their efforts.

Say: **Now lie down and push yourself up off the floor with your arms.** Have children do a few push-ups and then return to a sitting position.

Say: **Now lean forward and touch your toes, then lie back down on the floor.** Have children do a few sit-ups.

Say: **God created us. He made our bodies. All the strength we have comes from God.**

3. Breakaway Buddies

(You'll need a Bible and toilet paper.)
Say: **You're very strong.** Ask:

● **Who gives you strength?** Let children respond, "Gods does."

● **Should we ever use our strong healthy bodies to hit or shove people? Why?**

Open the Bible to Judges 13 and show it to the children. Say: **Samson made some people very mad at him and they wanted to catch him and kill him. They tried to trick him by waiting until he was asleep and tying him up. It didn't work because Samson was so strong that when he woke up he broke the ropes and escaped.**

Samson had a special secret for being so strong. He knew it was dangerous to tell anyone what it was, but he told his girlfriend his secret anyway. She told Samson's enemies, and they made another plan to catch him. Before I tell you what that plan was, let's pretend we're as strong as Samson.

Form pairs and give each pair a roll of toilet paper. Have children pretend the toilet paper is rope. Have one partner tie up the other, and then let the tied-up partner break out of the "ropes." Then have partners switch, and let the second partner break out of the ropes.

Say: **You really did a great job breaking out of those ropes! God gave you that strength, just like he gave Samson his strength. All our strength comes from God.**

4. Samson's Secret

(You'll need two stacks of empty cardboard boxes or blocks, at least 3 feet tall.)

Say: **Samson forgot that God gives us strength, and he told his girl-**

friend that God gave him strength as long as he didn't cut his hair. She waited until he was sleeping, and then she called in one of the men who hated Samson, and he cut off Samson's hair. Men came and captured Samson, and this time Samson couldn't get away. God had taken all his strength away from him. Ask:

● **Where did Samson's strength come from in the first place?**

Say: **The men were very mean to Samson. They made him blind, and they kept him tied up where people could go by and make fun of him. These people were also being mean to the rest of the people in Samson's country. Samson was sorry he hadn't obeyed God. He knew that all his strength had come from God. He couldn't see anymore, and he couldn't escape.** Ask:

● **What could Samson do?**

Say: **Samson could pray and talk to God. Listen carefully to what Samson prayed: "Lord, just one more time, please make me strong. Please give me enough strength to stop these people who are being so mean to our people. I don't care if I die, too."**

Ask:

● **Do you think God heard Samson's prayer?**

Say: **Yes, God heard Samson's prayer. He forgave Samson and gave him back his strength. Samson was tied up between two large posts in the center of a big building. Lots of people were in the building making fun of him. He put his hands on the posts, and he began to push as hard as he could.**

Select one child to stand between the two stacks of cardboard boxes. Say: **Push the boxes like you think Samson might have pushed on those posts.**

Let several children push down the boxes. Then say: **That's the way Samson pushed and the posts broke and the building fell down and killed the mean people.** Ask:

● **How did God answer Samson's prayer?**

Say: **Samson's strength came from God. All our strength comes from God, too. We need to depend on him to help us do the things he wants us to do.**

5. Haircuts

(Before class, cut the centers out of paper plates. Cut brown yarn into 7-inch lengths in groups of five as illustrated below. Tie the bundles of five together in the middle. Make enough for each child to have three. You'll also need the stapler or tape, crayons, mirror, and scissors.)

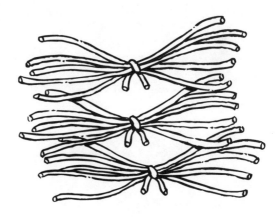

Seat children at tables. Give each child a rim from a paper plate and three bundles of yarn. Help children staple or tape the yarn to the outer edges of the plate. The yarn will hang down like hair. They may color the rim of the plate brown. Let them try on their "hair" and look at themselves in the mirror.

Now have children take the plates off their heads and cut the hair off with scissors. Have them tell you the story of Samson.

Say: **We don't get our strength from our hair. But we do get our strength from God. And he cares about all we do.**

6. Strong Treats

(You'll need licorice strings and paper towels.)

Have children clean off the tables from the "Haircuts" activity. Give each child a couple of strings of red licorice on a paper towel.

Say: **These licorice strings are kind of like the hair that the mean men cut off of Samson. Samson lost his strength when his hair was cut because he had promised God he would never cut his hair. God gives us strength when we obey him. Let's pray that we will always have strength because we always obey God.**

Pray a brief prayer thanking God for strength and for the treat. Then have children eat their licorice strings.

God Cares

Preschoolers can easily become frightened in strange places. They may even become uncomfortable when unfamiliar people appear in familiar places. They need the assurance that God is always with them and that he takes care of them wherever they go. Use this lesson to help kids remember that God is everywhere.

A POWERFUL POINT

"God heard the boy crying, and God's angel called to Hagar from heaven. He said, 'What is wrong, Hagar? Don't be afraid! God has heard the boy crying there. Help him up and take him by the hand. I will make his descendants into a great nation.' Then God showed Hagar a well of water. So she went to the well and filled her bag with water and gave the boy a drink" (Genesis 21:17-19).

Children will learn:
God takes care of us everywhere.

A LOOK AT THE LESSON

1. Taking a Trip (5 to 10 minutes)
2. Prayer Train (5 minutes)
3. Travel Prayers (5 minutes)
4. Moving Our Muscles (3 minutes)
5. Family Fights (5 minutes)
6. Travel Bags (10 minutes)
7. Moving On (5 minutes)
8. Wonderful Water (5 to 10 minutes)

THE FUN-TO-LEARN LESSON

1. Taking a Trip

(You'll need a hat, a coat, and a suitcase full of clothes.)

Greet the children by wearing a hat and coat and carrying a suitcase full of clothes. Say: **Today we're going to hear about a lady and her son who had to move away from their home. They weren't sure where they were going, but God went with them.**

Ask: **Have you ever moved away from a home?** Let children respond, then open your suitcase and let them play with the clothes.

2. Prayer Train

Say: **Let's travel on our train to Abraham's house and see what's happening. All aboard the prayer train!**

Prayer-Train Rhyme

All aboard the prayer train!
(Start slowly.) **Chug-a-chug, chug-a-chug.**
(Faster) **Chug-a-chug, chug-a-chug.**
Chug-a-chug-a-choo-choo.
Jesus loves you!
Chug-a-chug-a-chee-chee.
Jesus loves me!
Up and down, up and down.
Jesus' love is all around!
(Repeat until all the children have joined the train.)

(Begin slowing down.) **Chug-a-chug, chug-a-chug.**
(Slower) **Chug-a-chug, chug-a-chug ... Chooo.**

Have children gather in a circle on the floor.

3. Travel Prayers

(You'll need a Bible.)
Present the Bible. Say: **The Bible tells us a lot about God and prayer.** Lay the open Bible on the floor and ask:

● **Where do our prayers go?**
● **Where is God?**

Say: **God is with us wherever we go.**

Sing the "Where, When, What? Song" together.

Where, When, What? Song

(Sing to the tune of "Three Blind Mice.")
Where do we pray?
Right here, anywhere!
When do we pray?
Right now, anytime!

What do we pray about?
All things without a doubt!
That's how we all can pray to God,
So let's pray now.

Say: **We can pray to God wherever we go. He's always there to help us, even when we travel. Do you ever say travel prayers like "Lord, keep us safe in the car when we go to Grandma's house"? Let's pray today for someone who lives far away. Think of someone you travel to see.**

Let children suggest people they travel to see, then pray for those people.

After your prayer say: **God is with**

us to hear our prayers, but he is also with the people we prayed for and he can help them. God will help us wherever we are.

4. Moving Our Muscles

Say: **Hagar is a person in our Bible story. Our story is in Genesis chapter 21 in the Bible. Our bodies like to move, so let's stand up and pretend we're traveling to Hagar's house. First let's take an airplane. Everyone be an airplane and fly around the room.**

Next have the children walk around the room like they're on a bus, in a car, on a horse, or crawling, and then walk back to the circle.

Say: **No matter where we go God is with us. It doesn't matter if we fly or ride or crawl or walk—God takes care of us everywhere.**

5. Family Fights

(Before class, prepare the finger puppets from page 93. You'll also need a Bible.)

Say: **Now that we've traveled to Hagar's house let's knock on the door and see what's happening.**

Show children the Bible one more time to reinforce where you're getting your information.

Say: **The Bible tells us Hagar and her son Ishmael lived with Abraham and Sarah. Sarah saw Ishmael tease and argue with her son Isaac. Do you ever argue or fight with your brothers or sisters? Let's watch what Isaac and Ishmael were doing, and you tell me if this ever happens to you.**

Present the two puppets and continue with the following script.

Family Fighting

Puppet One: I want you to leave me alone! Don't touch me. I had that toy first. *(Let the puppets hit one another.)*

Puppet Two: That hurts! I'm going to tell on you. You shouldn't hit. *(Have puppet cry.)*

Puppet One: If you tell on me, I'll hit you again.

(Have puppets fight and cry some more, then put them away.)

Ask: **If you were their parents, what would you say to those boys right now?** Give several children a chance to share.

Say: **The boys Isaac and Ishmael fought so much God told Abraham it would be best if Hagar moved out of his house. So Abraham gave them some supplies and had them leave.**

Hagar and Ishmael had to walk a long way. They didn't have a car or even a horse. They got very tired walking, and they got very thirsty. They drank all the water they had, and they were still thirsty. Ishmael sat down and began to cry. They were far away from home, and they couldn't find water. There was no one around to help them. Do you think God was with them? Let's go pack our suitcases and go on a trip with Hagar and Ishmael to see what God did for them.

6. Travel Bags

(Before class, cut 2 inches off the top of each lunch bag. Cut the 2-inch wide loop open and fold the strip in half lengthwise, then cut it to about 10 inches long. This will make a 1×10-inch handle for each bag. Cut out magazine pictures of items children might pack if they were moving or traveling. You'll also need crayons and tape.)

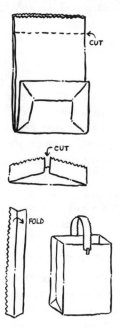

Gather the children around the tables. Give them paper lunch bags and handles. Let them decorate the bags and handles with crayons. Assist them in taping the handles on the bags.

Let children choose a few pictures to put in their travel bags. Let them draw their own pictures on scraps of paper to add to their bags while they wait for everyone to finish.

Say: **When we pack our bags, it usually means we're going some-where. And we put things in our bags we want to take with us. Do we need to put God in our bags to take him with us? No!**

God takes care of us everywhere. We can't pack him in our bags, but he'll be with us anyway!

Have kids form groups of three or four. In their groups, have each person tell the others, "God loves you. He's with you wherever you go." Choose one child in each group to start, and have kids go around their group to the right until all children have spoken to all the others.

7. Moving On

(Before class, hide a pitcher of water under a table or in a cupboard where children won't see it. The children need their travel bags.)

Say: **Let's take our bags and go for a long walk. We're thirsty, and we're looking for water.** If possible, walk the children through the halls of the building.

Say: **Let's sing a song that will help us as we travel.**

Wherever I Go

(Sing to the tune of "Here We Go 'Round the Mulberry Bush.")
God is with me wherever I go,
Wherever I go,
Wherever I go.
God is with me wherever I go.
He takes care of me, I know! (*Have children shout, "I know!"*)

Sing this song several times as you walk around looking for water. Return to your room and stop the children near the hidden water, but don't reveal it to the children yet.

Say: **Let's sit down here and find out what happened to Hagar and Ishmael. The Bible says that Hagar prayed to God for help and an angel answered her. The angel told her** **God was with them and he would make sure they could find water and a new place to live. Just then Hagar saw a well full of water where she could get a drink for them. She was so happy. I'm sure she thanked God for being with them and taking care of them.**

Ask:
● **Where does God take care of us?**
● **Where is God right now?**

Say: **God is right here with us, and he takes care of us wherever we go. Are you thirsty? Let's see if we can find water to drink.**

8. Wonderful Water

(You'll need the pitcher of water, Kool-Aid mix, stirring spoon, picnic blanket, cups, and popcorn. The children will need their travel bags.)

Say: **Let's search around and see if we can find a pitcher of water.** Help the children find the water. Let them put the Kool-Aid mix in the water and stir it up.

Say: **Our treat time can be a picnic.** Place the picnic blanket on the floor and have the children sit down. Have them take the magazine pictures out of their travel bags and give them popcorn to put in the bags. Give each child a cup of Kool-Aid and say the treat-time prayer together: **Now it's time to have my treat. Thank you, God, for food to eat.**

Enjoy your picnic. Remind children that God is with them wherever they go.

FINGER PUPPETS

Fun-to-Learn Songs

These are the fun songs and rhymes from *Fun-to-Learn Bible Lessons.* They are designed to help your children learn biblical truths. Use this song sheet to help your children remember favorite songs and rhymes from the lessons.

Prayer-Train Rhyme

All aboard the prayer train!
(Start slowly.) **Chug-a-chug, chug-a-chug.**
(Faster) **Chug-a-chug, chug-a-chug. Chug-a-chug-a-choo-choo. Jesus loves you! Chug-a-chug-a-chee-chee. Jesus loves me! Up and down, up and down. Jesus' love is all around!**
(Repeat until all the children have joined the train.)
(Begin slowing down.) **Chug-a-chug, chug-a-chug.**
(Slower) **Chug-a-chug, chug-a-chug...Chooo.**

Where, When, What? Song

(Sing to the tune of "Three Blind Mice.")
Where do we pray?
Right here, anywhere!
When do we pray?
Right now, anytime!

What do we pray about?

All things without a doubt!
That's how we all can pray to God,
So let's pray now.

I Can Trust

(Sing to the tune of "Mary Had a Little Lamb.")
I can trust the Bible,
The Bible, the Bible.
I can trust the Bible
Because it is God's Word.

I Will Listen

(Sing to the tune of "Frère Jacques.")
I will listen. I will listen.
God is near. God is near.
We can listen for him. We can listen for him.
We will hear. We will hear.

Fall, Wall!

(Sing to the tune of "Pop! Goes the Weasel.")
All around the wall they marched.
Yes, Joshua led the people.
They heard God's call to make it fall.
Crash! Went the wall.

Helping-Hands Rhyme

See my hands. They help me so.
(Hold up both hands.)
Wiggly fingers—watch them go!
(Wiggle fingers.)

When I talk to God, I pray.
Each one tells me what to say.
(Fingers of one hand touch the other hand.)

Thumbs are, oh, so close to me.
(Touch thumbs to chest.)
I'll pray for my family.

Pointer tells me what to do. *(Shake index finger.)*
I'll pray for my teacher, too.

Middle stands so tall, not bent.
(Hold one hand upright and hold the other hand flat over it.)
I'll pray for the president.

This one likes to wear a ring. *(Hold up fourth finger.)*
For the sick and weak, I'll sing.

Little finger—small to see. *(Wiggle pinkie.)*
Now, I think, I'll pray for me.

See, my hands—they help me so.
(Fold hands in prayer.)
Fold together with heads bowed low.

Thank You Song

(Sing to the tune of "Row, Row, Row Your Boat.")
Thank you, thank you, thank you, God.
Thank you from my heart.
Thank you, thank you, thank you, God.
Thank you from my heart.

Wherever I Go

(Sing to the tune of "Here We Go 'Round the Mulberry Bush.")
God is with me wherever I go,
Wherever I go,
Wherever I go.
God is with me wherever I go.
He takes care of me, I know!

Evaluation of *Fun-to-Learn Bible Lessons: Preschool, Volume 2*

Please help Group Publishing, Inc., continue providing innovative and usable resources for ministry by taking a moment to fill out and send us this evaluation. Thanks!

● ● ●

1. As a whole, this book has been (circle one):

Not much help   Very helpful

1   2   3   4   5   6   7   8   9   10

2. The things I liked best about this book were:

3. This book could be improved by:

4. One thing I'll do differently because of this book is:

5. Optional Information:

Name _____

Street Address _____

City _____ State _____ Zip _____

Phone Number _____ Date _____